THE
HALLOUMI
COOKBOOK

HarperCollins*Publishers*
1 London Bridge Street
London SE1 9GF

www.harpercollins.co.uk

First published by HarperCollins*Publishers* 2018

3 5 7 9 10 8 6 4 2

© HarperCollins*Publishers* 2018

Photographer: Joff Lee
Food Stylist: Mari Williams
Prop Stylist: Joanna Harris

Heather Thomas asserts the moral right to be identified as the author of this work

A catalogue record of this book is available from the British Library

HB ISBN 978-0-00-830092-0
EB ISBN 978-0-00-830093-7

Printed and bound in Latvia

MIX
Paper from
responsible sources
FSC C007454
www.fsc.org

FSC™ is a non-profit international organisation established to promote the
responsible management of the world's forests. Products carrying the FSC
label are independently certified to assure consumers that they come from
forests that are managed to meet the social, economic and ecological needs
of present and future generations, and other controlled sources.

Find out more about HarperCollins and the environment at
www.harpercollins.co.uk/green

THE
HALLOUMI
COOKBOOK

HEATHER THOMAS

HarperCollinsPublishers

CONTENTS

//

INTRODUCTION

//

In recent years, halloumi has become one of the most popular
cheeses in the world. What makes it so special is its high melting
point, and is sometimes simply referred to as 'grilling cheese'.
Unlike other cheeses, it is really versatile and can be grilled (broiled),
griddled, barbecued, fried, roasted or baked without melting or
losing its shape. Crisp and appetizingly golden brown on the outside,
yet tender inside, it has a firm, and 'meaty', albeit slightly rubbery
and 'squeaky', texture. Together with its salty, tangy, umami flavour,
this makes it different from any other cheese, as does its ability
to keep well in the fridge for up to a year if it's left sealed
in brine in its original packaging.

HISTORY AND ORIGINS

Although a recent phenomenon for many, halloumi isn't new – it's been around for centuries. The name is derived from the medieval Egyptian Arabic *halom* and in Turkey it's still known as *hellim*. It originated over 1,000 years ago in Cyprus where it was a valuable source of protein for poor agrarian communities living off the land. Each village had its own special recipe and this semi-hard, unripened white cheese was made communally from sheep's milk. As time passed, goat's milk was sometimes added too, and some modern versions are even made with cow's milk, although purists frown on this practice.

Mint was usually added for flavour, and the cheese keeps better when it is wrapped in fresh mint leaves. The halloumi most of us buy tends to be younger and milder than the dry, salty unpasteurised varieties that are still eaten in Cyprus where it is aged in brine for much longer to intensify the taste.

NUTRITION

Halloumi is rich in protein, vitamin A and calcium. Although, like other cheeses, it is relatively high in fat you can buy reduced-fat versions with 40 per cent less fat. And because most halloumi is made with goat's or sheep's milk it's much lower in lactose than cow's milk cheeses and can often be tolerated by people with mild lactose intolerance. It is higher in salt than most cheeses (330mg sodium per 25g/1oz), so if you're on a low-sodium diet for health reasons, it would be wise to limit your consumption and to eat it in smaller quantities.

COOKING WITH HALLOUMI

Halloumi is widely eaten throughout Greece, Turkey and the Levant as a meze (a selection of small dishes served with drinks or at the start of a meal) or for breakfast, usually with hummus or falafels, or watermelon, olives and freshly baked bread in the hot summer months. In Cyprus, the Greek islands and mainland Greece it is used (pan-seared or fried) to make *saganaki* or served in salads and with grilled vegetables or *lountza*, a spiced smoked pork sausage. Its distinctive saltiness is a good counterpoint to the sweetness of watermelon, melon, figs and citrus fruits.

The recipes in this book include the latest trends as well as classic dishes from the eastern Mediterranean: Cyprus, Greece, Turkey, Lebanon, Syria, Egypt and Israel. Many are augmented with Middle Eastern flavourings and spices, such as preserved lemons, pomegranate molasses, sumac and za'atar. In addition, we have new and innovative recipes for halloumi sliders, 'fries', 'fingers', 'bites', burgers and fritters. It's so versatile that it can be cooked over hot coals on a barbecue, griddled as a base for bruschetta, baked in pies or used as a topping for pizza. There are toasties, wraps and sandwiches plus great ideas for breakfast and brunch. We even have a vegetarian recipe for crisp battered halloumi 'fish and chips'.

Whereas many of the recipes are vegetarian – often incorporating healthy grains, pulses and pasta – chicken, meat and fish are also featured. We even have a special section dedicated to baking with halloumi with recipes for delicious loaves, savoury scones and cheesy muffins. This is the ultimate cookbook for everyone who loves halloumi and wants to eat a really nutritious and healthy diet.

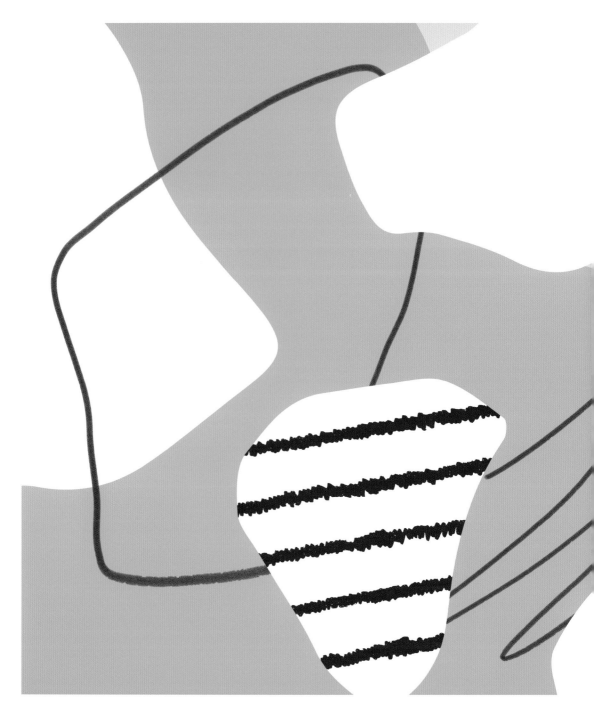

BASIC RECIPES

BAKED HALLOUMI

Instead of frying halloumi, why not bake it in the oven? It's so easy, especially if you already have the oven on. Or you can scatter it, sliced or diced, over some roasted vegetables, a rice or pasta bake or a dish of beans or lentils for the last 10–15 minutes of the cooking time.

Preheat the oven to 200°C (180°C fan)/400°F/gas 6.

Cut the halloumi into slices, about 1–2cm (½ –¾ inch) thick, and arrange them on a baking tray (cookie sheet). Spray lightly with olive oil or drizzle some over the top. For additional flavour, you can sprinkle with some herbs, spices or crushed seeds, or drizzle with honey.

Cook in the hot oven for 10–15 minutes until crisp and uniformly golden brown.

Eat immediately before the halloumi cools down.

SERVING SUGGESTIONS
- Dust with ground spices, such as sumac, cumin or paprika (sweet or smoked).
- Sprinkle with dried or fresh herbs, e.g. oregano, thyme, chopped rosemary.
- Drizzle with pomegranate molasses, balsamic vinegar or glaze.
- Squeeze some lemon juice over the top.
- Drizzle with honey.
- Serve as an appetizer with roasted or char-grilled red (bell) peppers (freshly cooked or bottled).
- Lay some thinly sliced halloumi over the top of an ovenproof dish of vegetables, a moussaka, pasta bake or pizza for the last 10–15 minutes of cooking for a crusty, cheesy topping.
- Add to bruschetta or crostini.

GRILLED (BROILED) OR GRIDDLED HALLOUMI

Halloumi looks good when it's cooked on a ridged griddle pan because it gives those appetizing char lines. If you don't have a griddle pan, cook it under a grill (broiler). You don't need to use oil when using this cooking method. Try the halloumi with one or more of the dips on pages 14–15.

USING A GRIDDLE PAN

Cut the halloumi into slices, about 1–2cm (½ –¾ inch) thick.

Set a ridged griddle pan over a medium heat and when it's hot, add the halloumi.

Dry-fry for 2–3 minutes each side until crisp, golden and attractively striped. Don't overcook or it will become too charred.

Remove from the pan with a slotted spoon or spatula and eat immediately. If you leave it to cool down, it may become rubbery.

USING A GRILL (BROILER)

Preheat the grill (broiler) to medium to high heat.

Arrange the slices of halloumi in a grill (broiler) pan (drizzle with olive oil if wished) and cook under the hot grill (broiler) for 2–3 minutes each side until crisp and golden brown.

Alternatively, place the cheese slices in a heatproof dish under the grill (broiler).

TZATZIKI

SERVES 6
PREP 10 MINUTES
DRAIN 30 MINUTES

1 large cucumber, peeled
 and halved
500g (1lb 2oz/2 cups) thick
 strained yoghurt, preferably
 goat's or sheep's milk
2 tbsp fruity green olive oil
3–4 garlic cloves, crushed
a small bunch of mint, finely
 chopped
a good squeeze of lemon juice
sea salt and freshly ground
 black pepper

Scoop out the seeds from the cucumber and discard them.
Dice the cucumber and put it in a colander with a little sea salt.
Leave to drain for about 30 minutes to extract most of the juice.
Squeeze and pat dry with kitchen paper (paper towels).

In a bowl, mix the cucumber into the yoghurt and olive oil. Stir
in the garlic and mint. Add lemon juice, salt and pepper to taste.

VARIATIONS
• Use dill instead of mint.
• Grate the cucumber instead of dicing it.

TAHINI DIP

SERVES 4
PREP 10 MINUTES

4 tbsp tahini
3 garlic cloves, crushed
a pinch of ground cumin
2 tbsp olive oil
juice of 1 small lemon
200g (7oz/scant 1 cup) thick
 strained Greek yoghurt
runny honey, for drizzling
a few sprigs of dill, chopped
sea salt

Whisk together the tahini, garlic, cumin, olive oil and lemon
juice in a bowl.

Stir in the yoghurt and season to taste. If the mixture is too
thick, you can add a spoonful of water to thin it a little. Cover
and chill in the fridge before serving, drizzled with honey and
sprinkled with dill.

VARIATIONS
• Sprinkle with shredded spring onions (scallions).
• Scatter with toasted sesame seeds.

SMOKY RED PEPPER AND AUBERGINE DIP

SERVES 4–6
PREP 10 MINUTES
COOK 25–30 MINUTES

1 large aubergine (eggplant)
3 red (bell) peppers
olive oil, for brushing
3 garlic cloves, crushed
½ tsp smoked paprika
½ tsp ground cumin
juice of ½ lemon
200g (7oz/scant 1 cup)
    0% fat Greek yoghurt
a few sprigs of coriander
    (cilantro), chopped
sea salt and freshly ground
    black pepper

Preheat the oven to 180°C (160°C fan)/350°F/gas 4.

Cook the whole aubergine (eggplant) and peppers in a griddle pan set over a medium to high heat for 5–10 minutes, turning occasionally, until charred and starting to soften.

Place the vegetables on a lightly oiled baking tray (cookie sheet) and roast in the oven for about 20 minutes until really tender. Leave to cool.

Scoop the aubergine (eggplant) out of the skin and place in a food processor. Skin and deseed the peppers and add to the food processor with the garlic, paprika, cumin and lemon juice. Blitz until smooth and transfer to a bowl. Season to taste and stir in the yoghurt and coriander (cilantro).

VARIATIONS
- Add some crushed chilli flakes, a diced red chilli or a dash of harissa.
- Stir in a little tahini or tomato paste.

FRIED HALLOUMI

Frying is the simplest and quickest way of cooking halloumi and the wonderful thing is that, unlike other cheeses, it does not melt. You can even dry-fry it to avoid adding extra fat if you are watching your weight. Don't worry if some of the brine in the cheese comes out into the pan while it's cooking – it will evaporate and you'll still end up with crisp and crusty golden halloumi slices, which are tender inside.

DRY-FRYING

Simply cut the block of cheese into slices – as thick as you like. This could be anything from 1–2cm (½ –¾ inch) thick.

Dry-fry in a non-stick frying pan (skillet) over a medium heat for 1–2 minutes each side until any liquid has been released and evaporated and the halloumi is golden brown and crispy on the outside and softened inside.

Remove from the pan with a slotted spoon or spatula and eat immediately. If you leave it to cool down, it may become rubbery.

FRYING IN OIL AND/OR BUTTER

You can fry halloumi in a little olive oil, which will enhance the flavour, as does unsalted butter. Just heat the oil and/or butter in a frying pan and cook as for dry-frying.

Note: Some people dust the halloumi with flour or semolina before frying to give it a deliciously crisp crust. You can even dip the slices into beaten egg first and then coat them with sesame seeds or crushed fennel or cumin seeds.

SERVING SUGGESTIONS

///

- Drizzle with some fruity green olive oil and freshly squeezed lemon juice.

- Use basil oil instead of regular olive oil.

- Drizzle some warm runny honey over the top and sprinkle with black or white sesame seeds.

- Sprinkle with finely chopped mint, coriander (cilantro), basil or flat-leaf parsley. Alternatively, dust with dried oregano or thyme.

- Scatter a pinch of crushed chilli flakes over the top to give it a kick.

- Dust with ground spices, e.g. paprika, cayenne, za'atar or sumac.

- Serve with a spoonful of chilli jam, fig jam or your favourite chutney.

- If you're not a purist, add a shake of hot sauce, e.g. Sriracha or Thai sweet chilli sauce, or a little harissa (regular or rose flavoured).

- Eat for breakfast with some fresh watermelon, peaches, pears or clementines. The juiciness and sweetness of the fruit complement its salty flavour perfectly.

- Serve with figs – fresh or oven-baked with honey.

- Add some peppery salad leaves, such as rocket (arugula) or watercress and drizzle with olive oil and balsamic vinegar.

- Wrap in wafer thin slices of prosciutto.

- Serve with some tahini or cooling tzatziki (see page 14).

- Serve on skewers with a spicy dip or lemony salsa.

- Be like the Greeks and eat it with a glass of chilled ouzo on ice.

GREEK FRIED HALLOUMI WITH OUZO

///

In Greece, fried halloumi is often served as a snack or an appetizer with drinks or as part of a mixed meze (a selection of small dishes served at the start of a meal). If wished, you can omit the ouzo in this recipe and serve the fried halloumi with lemon juice only.

SERVES 4
PREP 2 MINUTES
COOK 3–5 MINUTES

2 tbsp extra-virgin olive oil
25g (1oz/2 tbsp) unsalted butter
4 slices of halloumi, about 2cm
    (¾ inch) thick
plain (all-purpose) flour,
    for dusting
3 tbsp ouzo
juice of 1 lemon

Heat the olive oil and butter in a frying pan (skillet) set over a medium heat.

Dust the halloumi lightly with flour and add to the pan when it's really hot.

Cook for 1–2 minutes each side until golden brown and crisp.

Pour the ouzo over the halloumi and set it alight. Stand back until the flames die down and then remove with a slotted spoon or spatula and serve while piping hot, drizzled with lemon juice.

BARBECUED HALLOUMI

//

Halloumi tastes especially good when cooked over hot coals or wood on a barbecue until it's slightly charred and crisp. It acquires a distinctive smoky flavour, which is complemented by spicy relishes, chutneys and sauces.

Light the barbecue grill and wait for it to get medium to hot and the flames to die down.

Cut the halloumi into slices or large cubes (not too small or they will fall through the bars of the grill).

Spray the halloumi lightly with oil to prevent it sticking.

Place the halloumi on the hot grill and cook for 2–3 minutes each side until slightly charred and crisp. Remove and eat immediately.

VARIATIONS
- Marinate the halloumi before cooking in a mixture of olive oil, lemon or lime juice, fresh thyme, mint, rosemary or oregano leaves and crushed garlic. Use to baste the cheese while it's cooking.
- You could also use a spicy tandoori yoghurt marinade.
- Wrap the halloumi in kitchen foil – you can add vegetables, herbs, diced chilli, etc. – before placing on the hot barbecue.

SERVING SUGGESTIONS
- Serve with rose harissa or a chilli-spiked relish.
- Place on top of a grilled burger in a bun with tomato ketchup and dill pickles.
- Substitute barbecued halloumi slices for a burger bun.
- Use as a base for a stack of roasted or barbecued vegetables.

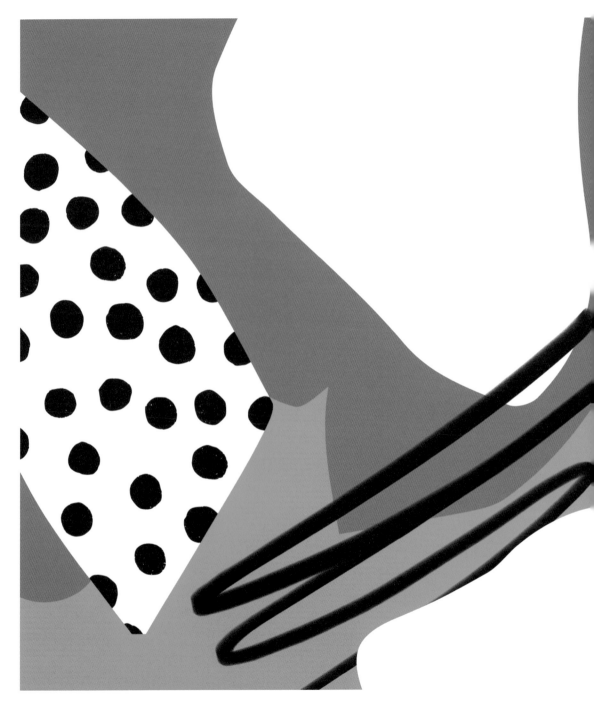

MEZE AND SNACKS

HALLOUMI FRIES WITH CARAMELISED BALSAMIC DRIZZLE

Caramelised balsamic vinegar adds a sharp sweetness to the halloumi fries. It's very easy to make and infinitely versatile. You can add a little to good olive oil for serving with fresh bread or drizzle it over roasted vegetables, lightly steamed greens or broccoli or some creamy soft goat's cheese. It's worth making three or four times the quantity in this recipe and bottling it. It will keep well for several months in the fridge or a cool place.

SERVES 4
PREP 5 MINUTES
COOK 10-12 MINUTES

4 tbsp balsamic vinegar
2 tsp (soft) brown sugar
2 tbsp olive oil, plus extra
    for frying
340g (12oz) halloumi
3 tbsp plain (all-purpose) flour
2 tsp smoked paprika

Put the balsamic vinegar and sugar in a small pan and set over a low heat. Stir gently until the sugar dissolves and then turn up the heat and bring to the boil. Reduce the heat to low and cook gently until syrupy, reduced and starting to caramelise. Remove from the heat.

After 2–3 minutes stir in the olive oil until well amalgamated and smooth. Set aside while you fry the halloumi.

Cut the halloumi into 12 'fingers' and dust them lightly with the flour and smoked paprika.

Spray a large frying pan (skillet) with olive oil or just add 1–2 tablespoons of oil and set over a medium to high heat.

When the oil is hot, add the halloumi in batches and fry for about 2 minutes each side until crisp and golden brown.

Remove the halloumi and drain on kitchen paper (paper towels) before arranging them on a serving plate. Drizzle with the balsamic mixture and eat immediately.

VARIATIONS
- Instead of drizzling the halloumi with balsamic vinegar, use ready-made balsamic glaze.
- Or blend 1 tablespoon of pomegranate molasses with the juice of ½ lemon or lime and 1 teaspoon runny honey and use as a drizzle.
- You can even substitute Thai sweet chilli sauce or your favourite fiery hot sauce.

GRIDDLED HALLOUMI BRUSCHETTA

If you want to make this even healthier you can omit the bread and use the griddled halloumi as a base for the aubergine (eggplant) and salsa topping. To reduce the fat and calories, use a 'low fat' or 'less fat' brand of halloumi. If you don't like tapenade, use green pesto instead.

SERVES 4
PREP 10 MINUTES
COOK 15 MINUTES

olive oil, for brushing
1 small aubergine (eggplant),
    sliced into rounds
250g (9oz) halloumi, cut into
    8 slices
8 slices of crusty baguette
1 garlic clove, halved
2 tbsp black olive tapenade

GRIDDLED TOMATO SALSA
6 cherry tomatoes
¼ red onion, finely chopped
a few sprigs of basil, chopped
1 tbsp olive oil
juice of ½ lemon
a few drops of balsamic vinegar
sea salt and freshly ground
    black pepper

Brush a ridged griddle pan with olive oil and set over a medium heat. When it's hot, add the aubergine (eggplant) and cook for about 2 minutes each side until softened, golden and attractively striped. Remove and drain on kitchen paper (paper towels). Keep warm.

Make the griddled tomato salsa: add the tomatoes to the hot griddle pan and cook for 3–4 minutes, turning occasionally, until starting to soften and char. Remove the tomatoes from the pan and chop coarsely. Mix with the other ingredients in a bowl and season to taste with salt and pepper.

Lay the slices of halloumi on the hot griddle and cook, in batches, for 2–3 minutes each side until crisp, golden and attractively striped. Don't overcook or it will become too charred.

Rub the baguette slices with the cut garlic clove. Brush some more olive oil over the griddle pan and lightly toast the bread for 1–2 minutes each side.

Spread the toasted bread with the tapenade and top with the sliced aubergine (eggplant) and halloumi. Place a spoonful of the griddled tomato salsa on top and serve immediately while everything is still hot.

HALLOUMI FRIES WITH HARISSA YOGHURT

//

Halloumi fries have really taken off and become a 'go to' food. Quick and easy to prepare and cook, you can flavour them with Middle Eastern spices, such as za'atar, sumac and ras-el-hanout, or even cayenne and chilli if you want to give them some heat. You can serve them simply with yoghurt or chilli sauce or a variety of dips – tzatziki or tahini (see page 14), a spicy salsa or guacamole.

SERVES 4
PREP 10 MINUTES
COOK 6–8 MINUTES

340g (12oz) halloumi
60g (2oz/½ cup) plain
   (all-purpose) flour
2 tbsp za'atar
vegetable oil for shallow-frying
1 tsp sumac
1 tbsp pomegranate molasses
a small bunch of mint or
   coriander (cilantro),
   coarsely chopped
seeds of 1 pomegranate

HARISSA YOGHURT
150g (5oz/⅔ cup)
   0% fat Greek yoghurt
2 tsp harissa

Make the harissa yoghurt: put the yoghurt in a small bowl and gently swirl in the harissa.

Cut the halloumi into fingers, about the size of fat potato chips. Sift the flour into a bowl and mix in the za'atar. Dip the halloumi fingers into the seasoned flour to coat them all over, shaking off any excess.

Add enough oil to cover the bottom of a large frying pan (skillet) and set over a medium to high heat. When it's hot, fry the halloumi fingers in batches for about 3–4 minutes, turning them until crisp and golden brown on both sides. Remove with a slotted spoon and drain on kitchen paper (paper towels). Lightly dust with the sumac.

Arrange the halloumi fries on a serving plate. Drizzle the harissa yoghurt and pomegranate molasses over the top and sprinkle with the herbs and pomegranate seeds. Serve immediately while the fries are really hot and crisp.

BARBECUED HALLOUMI PITTA POCKETS

//

Marinating the halloumi before grilling it over wood or hot coals enhances the flavour. If you don't have a barbecue or seasonal weather conditions make cooking outdoors unappealing, stay inside in the warm and use a griddle pan instead. You can still crisp and char the halloumi and give it a smoky kick.

SERVES 4
PREP 15 MINUTES
COOK 15 MINUTES

340g (12oz) halloumi, thickly
    sliced
olive oil, for brushing
1 large red onion, cut into wedges
1 yellow (bell) pepper
1 red (bell) pepper
4 pitta breads
a handful of wild rocket (arugula)
4 heaped tbsp Greek yoghurt
pomegranate molasses or
    balsamic vinegar, for drizzling
sea salt and freshly ground
    black pepper

ROSE HARISSA MARINADE
2 tbsp olive oil
juice of 1 lemon
2 tsp rose harissa paste

Mix the ingredients for the rose harissa marinade in a bowl and add the halloumi, turning it until well coated in the marinade.

Fire up the barbecue and when it's really hot and the flames die down lightly oil the grill.

Add the red onion wedges and peppers and cook for about 8–10 minutes or until softened and slightly charred. Remove and keep warm.

Add the halloumi and cook for about 2 minutes each side until golden brown and slightly charred. Remove and keep warm.

Place the pitta breads on the oiled grill and cook for about 30 seconds each side. Remove and keep warm.

Peel the peppers when they are cool enough to handle and remove the inner ribs and seeds. Cut into slices.

Make a slit along one side of each pitta bread and open it up. Fill with the rocket (arugula), grilled onions, peppers and halloumi. Add a spoonful of yoghurt to each pitta and drizzle with pomegranate molasses or balsamic vinegar.

Tip: If you have a large barbecue you can grill the halloumi and pitta breads alongside the onions and peppers to speed things up.

VARIATIONS
· Add tzatziki (see page 14) or hummus instead of yoghurt.
· Use wraps or tortillas instead of pittas.

GRIDDLED HALLOUMI WITH WATERMELON SALSA

In mainland Greece and on the islands, grilled (broiled) halloumi is often eaten for breakfast with some fresh fruit, especially juicy figs or a slice of chilled watermelon. It's refreshing and cooling in the intense heat of a Greek summer. The sweetness and crunchiness of the melon complements the appetizingly charred cheese. We've taken this one step further and added the watermelon to a lightly spiced salsa and served it with griddled bread.

SERVES 4
PREP 10 MINUTES
COOK 10–12 MINUTES

1 tbsp green fruity olive oil,
    e.g. Kalamata
4 thick slices crusty bread
    or ciabatta
400g (14oz) halloumi,
    cut into 4 thick slices

WATERMELON SALSA
500g (18oz) peeled
    watermelon, cubed
¼ cucumber, diced
250g (9oz) multicoloured
    tomatoes, coarsely chopped
1 small bunch of spring onions
    (scallions), chopped
1 red chilli, diced
a handful of mint or basil,
    chopped
1 tbsp green fruity olive oil,
    e.g. Kalamata
juice of 1 lime or ½ lemon
sea salt and freshly ground
    black pepper

Make the watermelon salsa at least 1 hour in advance so you can serve it well chilled. Mix the watermelon, cucumber, tomatoes, spring onions (scallions), chilli, herbs, olive oil and lime or lemon juice together in a bowl. Season to taste but go easy on the salt as halloumi can be quite salty. Cover and chill in the fridge until ready to serve.

Just before serving, brush a ridged griddle pan with the olive oil and set over a medium heat. When the pan is really hot, add the bread and cook for about 1 minute each side – just long enough to toast it. Remove and keep warm.

Add the halloumi to the pan and cook for 2–3 minutes each side until golden brown and attractively striped on the outside and starting to soften inside.

Serve the hot halloumi and griddled bread immediately with the chilled watermelon salsa.

VARIATIONS
- Serve the watermelon salsa with feta or a creamy goat's cheese.
- Use Cantaloupe or Charantais melon instead of watermelon.
- For a hotter, more spicy salsa add another chilli and some coriander (cilantro).

STICKY GLAZED HALLOUMI BITES

Runny honey is traditionally used to make a glaze for halloumi, but pomegranate molasses is less sweet and has a more distinctive and intense flavour. It's made by reducing pomegranate juice to a syrup – you can do this yourself at home or buy it ready-made. If you have a sweet tooth, just add a tablespoon of honey to the glaze mixture.

SERVES 4–6
PREP 10 MINUTES
COOK 5–8 MINUTES

500g (18oz) halloumi
1 tbsp olive oil, plus extra
   for brushing
juice of 1 small lime
1 tsp ras-el-hanout
½ tsp za'atar
1 tbsp pomegranate molasses
1 tbsp white sesame seeds
a handful of coriander
   (cilantro), chopped

Cut the halloumi into 2.5cm (1 inch) cubes and thread them onto small bamboo skewers that have been soaked in water to prevent them burning. Add 2–3 cubes per skewer.

In a bowl, whisk together the olive oil, lime juice, spices and pomegranate molasses to make a sticky glaze.

Lightly brush the glaze over the halloumi cubes to cover them completely.

Lightly brush a ridged griddle pan with oil and place over a medium heat. When the pan is hot, add the halloumi skewers and cook, turning occasionally, for about 5–8 minutes until sticky, golden brown and glazed all over. Watch carefully and take care that they do not burn. Alternatively, you can bake them in the oven.

Arrange the skewers on a serving plate and sprinkle with sesame seeds and chopped coriander (cilantro). Serve immediately while they are still hot.

> Tip: If liked, you can remove the halloumi bites from the skewers before serving. However, it's easier to cook them on the skewers than loose in the pan.

SAGANAKI PAN-SEARED HALLOUMI

//

Wherever you go in Greece you will find saganaki on the menu, usually as a meze or an appetizer. The name is derived from the two-handled small frying pan (skillet) in which it is cooked – a saganaki. Halloumi works well as it has a higher melting point than other cheeses and keeps its shape better when fried.

SERVES 4
PREP 10 MINUTES
COOK 8–10 MINUTES

450g (1lb) halloumi, cut into
   thick slices
1 large free-range egg, beaten
6 tbsp semolina
3 tbsp olive oil
crusty bread or warm flatbreads,
   to serve

LEMON AND GARLIC DRESSING
2 tbsp fruity green olive oil
juice of 1 lemon
1 garlic clove, crushed
1 tbsp capers
a handful of mint or flat-leaf
   parsley

Make the lemon and garlic dressing: blitz all the ingredients in a blender until smooth.

Dip the halloumi into the beaten egg and then coat with the semolina, shaking off any excess.

Heat the olive oil in a large frying pan (skillet) set over a medium heat. When the oil is really hot, add the halloumi, a few slices at a time, and fry for about 2 minutes each side until golden brown, crisp and crusty. Remove and drain on kitchen paper (paper towels).

Serve the fried halloumi straight from the pan, drizzled with the lemon and garlic dressing and with some bread to soak up any leftover dressing.

VARIATIONS
· Drizzle with warm runny honey and sprinkle with black or white sesame seeds.
· Drizzle with freshly squeezed lemon juice and sprinkle with dried or fresh oregano.
· Use kefalotiri cheese instead of halloumi.

HALLOUMI AND PRAWN MINI BROCHETTES

//

Serve these little brochettes as a snack or party dish or even as an appetizer course.
A glass of chilled white wine or ouzo makes a great accompaniment. You can use frozen
raw prawns (shrimp) but make sure you defrost them thoroughly first.

SERVES 4
PREP 10 MINUTES
COOK 4-5 MINUTES

60ml (2fl oz/¼ cup) green
    olive oil
a handful of basil leaves
a good squeeze of lemon juice
24 unpeeled raw large prawns
    (jumbo shrimp)
275g (10oz) halloumi
12 woody rosemary stalks
    (optional)
a pinch of dried crushed
    chilli flakes
sea salt and freshly ground
    black pepper
warm pitta bread triangles,
    to serve

Put the olive oil, basil and lemon juice in a small blender or food
chopper and blitz until well blended and beautifully green. Season
with a little salt and pepper.

Peel the prawns, removing most of the shell but leaving the tails
on. Cut the halloumi into cubes.

Thread the prawns and halloumi onto 12 thin bamboo skewers
that have been soaked in water to prevent them burning.
Alternatively, strip most of the leaves from each rosemary
stalk, just leaving the green leafy tip, and use as skewers instead.

Brush the prawns and cheese lightly with a little of the basil oil.

Set a griddle pan over a medium heat and when it's hot add the
prawn and halloumi skewers. Cook, turning occasionally, for
4–5 minutes until the prawns have turned pink and are cooked
right through and the halloumi is golden brown.

Arrange on a serving plate and drizzle the remaining basil oil over
the top. Sprinkle with the chilli flakes and a little freshly ground
black pepper and serve hot with warm triangles of pitta bread
to mop up the oil.

VARIATION
· Use fresh coriander (cilantro) and lime juice to make the
herb flavoured oil.

BACON WRAPPED HALLOUMI NIBBLES WITH DIPS

Crispy bacon and tender halloumi are a winning combination for a snack or party canapé. Serve these nibbles with one or more of the yoghurt-based dips opposite or as a topping for a leafy salad with sprouting seeds and pine nuts.

SERVES 4–6
PREP 5 MINUTES
COOK 4–5 MINUTES

340g (12oz) halloumi
12 thin-cut rashers (slices)
    streaky bacon or pancetta
olive oil, for brushing
lemon juice, for sprinkling

Cut the halloumi into 12 fingers and then cut each one in half so you end up with 24 pieces.

Stretch out the bacon rashers by scraping the back of a knife along them until they are thinner and more elongated. Cut each one into two pieces. Wrap a bacon rasher around each piece of halloumi.

Lightly brush a non-stick frying pan (skillet) with olive oil and set over a medium heat. Add the bacon-wrapped halloumi to the hot pan and cook, turning occasionally, for 4–5 minutes until crisp and golden brown all over.

Serve immediately, sprinkled with lemon juice, before the bacon loses its crispness with one of the dips below.

Tip: For a lower-fat version, you can use wafer-thin slices of Parma ham instead of bacon or pancetta.

POMEGRANATE MOLASSES YOGHURT DIP

250g (9oz/1 cup) 0% fat
   Greek yoghurt
a small bunch of mint, chopped
seeds of 1 pomegranate
1 tbsp pomegranate molasses
sea salt and freshly ground
   black pepper

Mix together the yoghurt, mint and most of the pomegranate seeds in a bowl. Season to taste with salt and pepper and swirl in the pomegranate molasses to create a marbled effect. Sprinkle with the remaining pomegranate seeds.

SRIRACHA DIP

250g (9oz/1 cup) 0% fat
   Greek yoghurt
2 tbsp light mayonnaise
1 garlic clove, crushed
juice of ½ small lime
2–3 tsp Sriracha

Mix all the ingredients together in a bowl until smooth and creamy. Add the Sriracha to taste, depending on how much heat you want.

SPINACH PESTO DIP

150g (5oz/1 cup) frozen
   chopped spinach, thawed
250g (9oz/1 cup) 0% fat
   Greek yoghurt
grated zest of ½ lemon
3–4 tbsp green pesto
freshly ground black pepper

Squeeze any excess water out of the thawed spinach in a sieve and mix in a bowl with the yoghurt, lemon zest and pesto. Season to taste with black pepper.

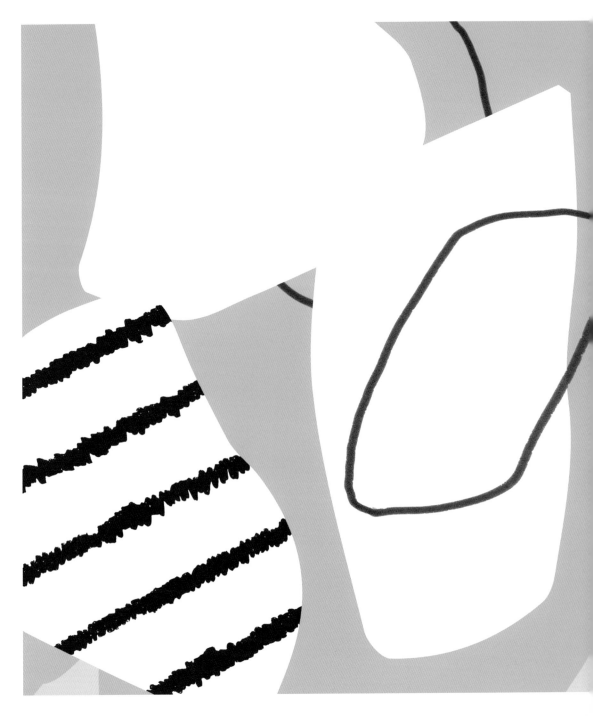

BRUNCHES

TURKISH SPICY SPINACH AND EGG BRUNCH

//

This is a really healthy and nutritious way to start the day. Everything is cooked in the same pan, so there's very little washing up. The fried halloumi adds crispness and perfectly complements the baked eggs and tender vegetables.

SERVES 4
PREP 10 MINUTES
COOK 15–20 MINUTES

2 tbsp olive oil
2 red onions, finely chopped
2 garlic cloves, crushed
1 red chilli, deseeded and diced
250g (9oz) halloumi, cubed
250g (9oz) baby plum tomatoes,
    halved
500g (1lb 2oz) baby spinach
    leaves
4 medium free-range eggs
200g (7oz/scant 1 cup) Greek
    yoghurt
smoked paprika, for dusting
a handful of dill or flat-leaf
    parsley, chopped
sea salt and freshly ground black
    pepper
toasted pittas or flatbreads,
    to serve

Heat the olive oil in a large frying pan (skillet) set over a medium heat. Add the onion, garlic and chilli to the hot pan and cook, stirring occasionally, for 6–8 minutes until starting to soften.

Add the halloumi and cook, stirring and turning, for about 2 minutes each side until it's crisp and golden brown.

Stir in the tomatoes and spinach and cook for 2–3 minutes until the spinach leaves wilt and the tomatoes are tender. Season to taste with salt and pepper.

Make four hollows in the mixture and crack the eggs into them. Reduce the heat to a bare simmer, as low as it will go, and cover the pan. Cook very gently for about 5 minutes until the whites of the eggs are set.

Add spoonfuls of the yoghurt to the pan in between the eggs and dust with smoked paprika. Sprinkle with the chopped herbs and serve immediately with toasted pittas or flatbreads.

HALLOUMI, HARISSA AND BACON TOASTS

Halloumi makes a satisfyingly substantial topping for a toastie due to its firm and almost 'meaty' texture. Drizzling it with honey or something equally sweet and syrupy is a good flavour counterpoint to the saltiness of the cheese.

SERVES 4
PREP 2 MINUTES
COOK 10–12 MINUTES

400g (14oz) halloumi, cut into 8 slices
8 thin-cut rashers (slices) streaky bacon or pancetta
4 thick slices of ciabatta or sourdough bread
olive oil, for brushing
2 tsp rose harissa
runny honey, for drizzling

Set a ridged griddle pan over a medium to high heat. When the pan is hot, add the halloumi and cook for 2–3 minutes each side until crisp and golden brown. Remove and keep warm.

Add the bacon to the pan and cook for about 2 minutes each side until golden brown and crispy. Remove and drain on kitchen paper (paper towels).

Brush the bread with olive oil and arrange in the hot pan. Toast for about 1–2 minutes on each side until lightly coloured.

Lightly spread the toasted bread slices with the rose harissa. Arrange the halloumi and crispy bacon on top and drizzle with honey. Serve immediately.

VARIATIONS
- Add some griddled cherry tomatoes, sliced (bell) peppers or mushrooms.
- Use a hot spicy chutney or chilli tomato jam instead of harissa.
- Drizzle with maple syrup, balsamic glaze or pomegranate molasses instead of honey.

HALLOUMI AND FRIED EGG BREAKFAST SANDWICH

This delicious toasted sandwich will energise you ahead of a busy day. Adding some hot sauce spices it up and complements the mildness of the halloumi.

SERVES 4
PREP 5 MINUTES
COOK 8–10 MINUTES

250g (9oz) halloumi,
    cut into 8 slices
2 tbsp olive oil, for frying
4 tomatoes, halved
4 medium free-range eggs
8 slices of multiseed or
    sourdough bread
a few chives, snipped
hot sauce, e.g. Sriracha or Thai
    sweet chilli, for drizzling
sea salt and freshly ground
    black pepper

Dry-fry the halloumi in a non-stick frying pan (skillet) over a medium heat for about 2 minutes each side until golden brown and crispy. Remove from the pan and set aside.

Add the olive oil to the hot pan and fry the tomatoes, cut-side down, for 2–3 minutes, just long enough to heat them through and soften them. Remove from the pan and set aside.

Break the eggs into the pan and fry until the whites are set and the yolks are still a little runny.

Meanwhile, lightly toast the bread. Arrange the tomatoes on four slices, season lightly with salt and pepper and top with the halloumi. Add a fried egg and sprinkle with chives. Drizzle with hot sauce and cover with the remaining slices of toast. Cut in half and serve immediately.

VARIATIONS
- Instead of hot sauce, add some tomato ketchup or even a spoonful of pesto.
- Add a few baby spinach leaves or some rocket (arugula).
- Fried mushrooms and crispy bacon are also good additions.

GRIDDLED HALLOUMI, SMOKED SALMON AND AVOCADO TOASTIES

Avocado toast is all the rage and a delicious way to kick-start the day. Topping it with smoked salmon and griddled halloumi transforms a simple snack into a more substantial brunch. Don't be put off by the fish and cheese combo – this works very well and tastes delicious.

SERVES 4
PREP 5 MINUTES
COOK 10 MINUTES

400g (14oz) halloumi, cut
   into 8 slices
4 thick slices of ciabatta
   or sourdough bread
olive oil, for brushing
2 small avocados, peeled
   and stoned
3 spring onions (scallions),
   finely chopped
a few chives, snipped
150g (5oz) thinly cut smoked
   salmon
juice of ½ lemon
freshly ground black pepper

Set a ridged griddle pan over a medium to high heat. When the pan is hot, add the halloumi and cook for 2–3 minutes each side until crisp and golden brown. Remove and keep warm.

Lightly brush the bread slices with olive oil and toast them in the hot pan for 1–2 minutes each side until lightly coloured.

Mash the avocados coarsely with a fork and mix in the spring onions (scallions) and chives. Spread over the toast and place the smoked salmon and griddled halloumi on top. Sprinkle with lemon juice and grind over some black pepper.

Serve immediately while the halloumi is still hot.

VARIATIONS
- Sprinkle some capers or diced dill pickles over the top.
- Use tarragon, dill or parsley instead of chives.
- For a more filling dish, top with a fried or poached egg.

SWEETCORN AND HALLOUMI FRITTERS

These delicious fritters are so quick and easy to make for a weekend brunch. Spice them up with a shake of hot chilli sauce or serve with poached or fried eggs for a more filling dish.

SERVES 4
PREP 15 MINUTES
COOK 6–8 MINUTES

75g (3oz/generous ½ cup)
    plain (all-purpose) flour
1 tsp baking powder
1 medium free-range egg
120ml (4fl oz/½ cup) milk
1 x 325g (11oz) can sweetcorn,
    drained
100g (4oz) halloumi, diced
1 red chilli, deseeded and diced
4 spring onions (scallions),
    finely chopped
a few sprigs of coriander
    (cilantro), chopped
2 tbsp olive oil
sea salt and freshly ground
    black pepper
sliced avocado, grilled (broiled)
    bacon and tomatoes, to serve

Sift the flour and baking powder into a large bowl. Beat in the egg and milk until you have a smooth batter. Stir in the sweetcorn, halloumi, chilli, spring onions (scallions) and coriander (cilantro). Season lightly with salt and pepper.

Heat the olive oil in a large non-stick frying pan (skillet) over a medium heat. When it's really hot, drop the batter, a few tablespoons at a time, into the pan and cook for about 2 minutes until set and golden brown underneath. Flip the fritters over and cook the other side for 1–2 minutes. Remove from the pan and drain on kitchen paper (paper towels). Keep warm while you cook the remaining fritters.

Serve the fritters with sliced avocado and crispy bacon and tomatoes.

BUTTERNUT SQUASH AND HALLOUMI FRITTATA

The great thing about a frittata is that it tastes equally good served hot, lukewarm or even cold. Enjoy it for brunch or a light supper, then wrap a wedge in some kitchen foil or cling film (plastic wrap) for a healthy packed lunch and take it to work with you.

SERVES 4
PREP 5 MINUTES
COOK 20 MINUTES

1 tbsp olive oil
450g (1lb) butternut squash,
    diced
2 garlic cloves, crushed
1 red chilli, deseeded and diced
150g (5oz) halloumi, thinly sliced
a handful of baby spinach leaves
6 free-range medium eggs
a handful of coriander (cilantro),
    chopped
freshly ground black pepper

Heat the olive oil in a large non-stick frying pan (skillet) set over a low to medium heat. Add the butternut squash to the hot pan and cook, stirring occasionally, for 8–10 minutes until tender.

Stir in the garlic, chilli, halloumi and spinach. Cook for about about 2–3 minutes, stirring occasionally, until the spinach wilts.

Beat the eggs and whisk in the coriander (cilantro) and some black pepper. Preheat the grill (broiler) on the high setting.

Pour the beaten eggs into the pan and cook gently over a low heat for about 5 minutes until the frittata is golden brown and set underneath.

Pop the pan under a preheated grill (broiler) for 4–5 minutes until the top is set, golden brown and puffed up.

Serve the frittata hot or lukewarm, cut into wedges.

VARIATIONS
• Use sweet potato or pumpkin instead of butternut squash.
• Make this spicier by adding some diced chorizo.

ROASTED VEGETABLES, HALLOUMI AND TAHINI BRUNCH

This colourful brunch is really nutritious and you can enjoy it for a light supper, too. If you don't want to make the tahini sauce, you could drizzle some green pesto over the vegetables and halloumi.

SERVES 4
PREP 15 MINUTES
COOK 25–30 MINUTES

400g (14oz) baby plum tomatoes
450g (1lb) sweet potatoes,
    scrubbed and cut into chunks
5 tbsp olive oil
20 asparagus stems, woody
    ends trimmed
340g (12oz) halloumi, cut
    into 8 slices
100g (4oz) baby spinach leaves
sea salt and freshly ground black
    pepper
warm flatbreads or pitta bread,
    to serve

TAHINI SAUCE
50g (2oz/scant ¼ cup) tahini
1 tsp runny honey
juice of ½ small lemon
1 garlic clove, crushed
a pinch of sea salt flakes
3 tbsp water

Preheat the oven to 190°C (170°C fan)/375°F/gas 5.

Arrange the tomatoes and sweet potatoes on a baking tray (cookie sheet). Drizzle with 3 tablespoons olive oil and season lightly with salt and pepper. Roast in the preheated oven for 25–30 minutes until tender.

Meanwhile, cook the asparagus in a pan of boiling water for 3–5 minutes until just tender (but not soggy). Drain and set aside to cool.

Make the tahini sauce: beat the tahini, honey, lemon juice, garlic and salt in a bowl until well combined. Whisk in the water, a spoonful at a time, to make a smooth sauce.

Set a ridged griddle pan over a medium heat. Toss the asparagus in the remaining olive oil and add to the hot pan. Cook for 3 minutes, turning occasionally, until hot and attractively striped with griddle lines. Remove and keep warm.

Add the halloumi to the pan and cook for about 2 minutes each side until crisp and golden brown.

Stir the baby spinach into the hot roast sweet potatoes and tomatoes. They will wilt slightly in the heat. Divide among four serving plates and top with the asparagus and halloumi. Drizzle with the tahini sauce and serve with warm flatbreads or pitta bread.

HALLOUMI QUESADILLAS WITH GUACAMOLE

///

If you've never considered making quesadillas with halloumi, think again. Crisp and golden on the outside with a hot, cheesy filling, they are the ultimate snack. You can even assemble them in advance and chill in the fridge for a few hours before cooking them. The number of chillies used depends on the variety (some are milder than others) and how much heat you like.

SERVES 4
PREP 15 MINUTES
COOK 6–8 MINUTES

250g (9oz) halloumi,
    coarsely grated
1 large red (bell) pepper,
    deseeded and diced
1 bunch of spring onions
    (scallions), thinly sliced
1–2 red chillies, diced
a large handful of coriander
    (cilantro), chopped
4 large flour tortillas
olive oil, for brushing

GUACAMOLE

1 red or green chilli, diced
½ red onion, diced
1 garlic clove, crushed
½ tsp sea salt crystals
2 ripe avocados, peeled
    and stoned
juice of 1 lime
1 ripe tomato, deseeded
    and diced
1 small bunch coriander
    (cilantro), chopped
freshly ground black pepper

Make the guacamole: crush the chilli, onion, garlic and salt in a pestle and mortar. Mash the avocados coarsely and stir in the lime juice, tomato, coriander and crushed onion mixture. Add a grinding of black pepper and set aside.

In a bowl, mix together the halloumi, red (bell) pepper, spring onion (scallions), chilli and coriander (cilantro).

Spread half the mixture over a tortilla, but not right up to the edge. Place another tortilla on top and press the halves together, especially the edges, to seal them. Repeat with the remaining filling and tortillas.

Lightly brush a non-stick frying pan (skillet) with olive oil and set over a medium heat. When the pan is hot, carefully add a quesadilla and cook for about 3 minutes until it's golden and crisp underneath. Use a spatula to flip it over and cook the other side. Slide out of the pan and keep warm while you cook the other quesadilla.

Serve the piping hot quesadillas, cut into wedges, with the guacamole.

> Tip: Instead of laying the tortillas on top of each other, you can spoon some filling onto half of each tortilla and then fold it over into a half moon shape. Press down firmly around the edge and cook as above.

LUNCHES

HALLOUMI-STUFFED FALAFELS IN PITTA POCKETS

//

These spicy falafels are bursting with flavour and so quick and easy to make. Adding diced halloumi makes them more substantial as well as adding texture. You can serve them with salad or even pop them into a sealed container and take them to work for a packed lunch.

SERVES 4
PREP 15 MINUTES
COOK 5–7 MINUTES

1 tsp cumin seeds
1 tsp coriander seeds
50g (2oz/generous ¼ cup)
    finely grated carrot
4 spring onions (scallions)
2 x 400g (14oz) cans chickpeas
    (garbanzo beans), rinsed
    and drained
1 red chilli, chopped
2 garlic cloves, peeled
grated zest of 1 lemon
1 small bunch of coriander
    (cilantro), finely chopped
2 tbsp plain (all-purpose) flour
½ tsp baking powder
175g (6oz) halloumi, diced
olive oil, for shallow frying
4 pitta breads
a handful of salad leaves
tahini, tzatziki (see page 14)
    or hummus, to serve
sea salt and freshly ground
    black pepper

Dry-fry the cumin and coriander seeds in a small pan over a medium heat for about 1 minute until they release their aroma. Take care not to let them burn.

Put the toasted seeds, carrot, spring onion (scallions), chickpeas (garbanzo beans), chilli, garlic, lemon zest, coriander (cilantro), flour, baking powder and seasoning in a food processor or blender and blitz until well combined but not smooth. The texture should still be slightly coarse.

Transfer the mixture to a bowl and stir in the halloumi, distributing it evenly throughout. Divide the mixture into 16 equal-sized portions and shape each one into a ball.

Heat the oil in a large frying pan (skillet) over a medium heat and add the falafels. Cook for about 2–3 minutes each side until golden brown. Remove from the pan and drain on kitchen paper (towels).

Meanwhile, toast the pitta breads or warm them in a lightly oiled griddle pan. Make a slit down one side of each pitta and open it up.

Fill the pittas with the salad leaves and falafels and drizzle with tahini or top with a dollop of tzatziki or hummus.

CARAMELISED RED ONION AND HALLOUMI TOASTIES

///

If you're in a hurry, instead of roasting these delicious toasties in the oven, divide the red onions, broccoli and halloumi among four large slices of seedy or multigrain bread and cover with the remaining slices. Brush with oil or melted butter and cook in a toasted sandwich maker or panini press. Or just fry in some butter in a frying pan (skillet) until slightly crisp and golden.

SERVES 4
PREP 10 MINUTES
COOK 20–25 MINUTES

2 tbsp olive oil, plus extra
    for drizzling
2 large red onions, thinly sliced
2 tbsp balsamic vinegar
1 tbsp (soft) brown sugar
200g (7oz) tenderstem
    broccoli, trimmed
8 slices of crusty bread or
    ciabatta
250g (9oz) halloumi, cut into
    8 slices
sea salt and freshly ground
    black pepper

Heat the olive oil in a frying pan (skillet) set over a low heat. Cook the onions, stirring occasionally, for about 5 minutes until they are starting to soften. Add the balsamic vinegar and sugar and cook for 5–10 minutes until meltingly soft and starting to caramelise. Season to taste with salt and pepper.

Meanwhile, cook the broccoli in a pan of boiling water for about 3 minutes until just tender. Drain well.

Preheat the oven to 200°C (180°C fan)/400°F/gas 6.

Lightly brush the bread on both sides with olive oil and place on a baking tray (cookie sheet). Top with the onion and lay the broccoli on top. Cover each one with a slice of halloumi and grind over a little black pepper.

Cook in the oven for about 10 minutes until the bread is toasted and crisp and the halloumi is golden brown and softened.

QUICK HALLOUMI TACOS WITH PICO DE GALLO

//

Jalapeño chilli peppers are very hot and spicy so if you prefer less heat, use some milder chillies instead. This recipe uses soft tortillas, but you can instead buy ready-made crisp taco shells in most supermarkets and delis.

SERVES 4
PREP 20 MINUTES
COOK 5 MINUTES

1 x 400g (14oz) can refried beans
60ml (2fl oz/¼ cup) soured
   cream
250g (9oz) halloumi, cut into
   8 slices
olive oil, for brushing
2 garlic cloves, crushed
4 large corn tortillas
1 ripe avocado, peeled, stoned
   and sliced
a few crisp iceberg lettuce leaves,
   shredded
soured cream and lime wedges,
   to serve

PICO DE GALLO
1 small red onion, finely chopped
1–2 jalapeño chillies, diced
2 juicy tomatoes, diced
a bunch of coriander (cilantro),
   chopped
juice of 1 lime
a pinch of sea salt crystals

Make the pico de gallo: mix all the ingredients together in a bowl, starting with one chilli and adding another if it's not hot enough for you. Set aside.

Heat the refried beans gently in a pan over a low heat or in the microwave. Stir in the soured cream to make the mixture creamy.

Brush the halloumi lightly with olive oil and cook in a frying pan (skillet) over a medium heat for 1–2 minutes each side until crisp and golden brown. Remove and drain on kitchen paper (paper towels).

Add the garlic to the hot pan and cook for about 30 seconds, without colouring. Remove immediately.

Warm the tortillas for about 30 seconds each side in the pan or on a hot griddle.

Assemble the tacos: put some refried beans on each tortilla with the avocado and lettuce, halloumi and garlic. Top with the pico de gallo and a little soured cream. Fold over and serve immediately with lime wedges.

Tip: If you can't find any fresh jalapeño chillies, use pickled ones.

VARIATIONS
• Add some diced fried crispy chorizo to the taco filling.
• Grill (broil) some vegetables (red onions and (bell) peppers) and add to the tacos.
• Serve with chunky guacamole.

HALLOUMI-STUFFED BAKED TOMATOES

//

You will need really large tomatoes for this traditional Greek dish. For the best flavour, serve it at room temperature. You can flavour the rice stuffing with some ground spices, such as cinnamon or cumin, or use mint instead of dill. Peppers can be stuffed in the same way and cooked alongside the tomatoes.

SERVES 4
PREP 15 MINUTES
COOK 1 HOUR 25 MINUTES

8 large beefsteak tomatoes
2 tbsp olive oil, plus extra
   for drizzling
1 red onion, finely chopped
2 garlic cloves, crushed
200g (7oz/generous 1 cup)
   long-grain rice (dry weight)
2 tsp tomato purée (paste)
135ml (4½fl oz/generous ½ cup)
   boiling vegetable stock
a handful of dill, chopped
85g (3oz/½ cup) pine nuts
85g (3oz/generous ½ cup)
   sultanas (golden raisins)
juice of 1 lemon
175g (6oz) halloumi, diced
sea salt and freshly ground
   black pepper
crusty bread, to serve

Preheat the oven to 200°C (180°C fan)/400°F/gas 6.

Slice the top off each tomato and set aside. Scoop out the seeds and pulp and place in a bowl. Arrange the tomato shells in a roasting pan and set aside.

Heat the olive oil in a frying pan (skillet) set over a low to medium heat. Cook the onion and garlic, stirring occasionally, for 8–10 minutes until tender and translucent – don't let them colour. Stir in the rice, tomato purée (paste), tomato seeds and pulp and the boiling stock.

Increase the heat and bring to the boil, then reduce the heat and cook for 10–12 minutes until the rice is starting to soften, but still retains a little bite. Stir in the chopped herbs, pine nuts, sultanas and lemon juice, and season to taste. Stir in the diced halloumi.

Divide the rice mixture among the tomato shells and cover with the reserved tops. Drizzle with olive oil and bake in the oven for about 1 hour until the tomatoes are soft and the rice is cooked and tender.

Serve warm or even cold with fresh crusty bread to mop up the delicious juices.

COURGETTI (ZUCCHINI) PASTA WITH FRIED HALLOUMI

The fried halloumi adds a crisp finishing touch to the lovely bright green pasta and courgetti (zucchini). If wished, you can make the green tahini sauce in advance and keep it in the fridge. If you don't have any linguine, spaghetti, angel hair pasta or even tagliatelle all work well.

SERVES 4
PREP 15 MINUTES
COOK 10–12 MINUTES

2 large courgettes (zucchini)
400g (14oz) linguine (dry weight)
olive oil, for spraying
250g (9oz) cherry or baby plum tomatoes, halved
1 tbsp balsamic vinegar
250g (9oz) halloumi, thinly sliced
toasted pine nuts, for sprinkling (optional)

GREEN TAHINI SAUCE
60g (2oz/¼ cup) tahini
2 garlic cloves, peeled
1 green chilli, deseeded
50g (2oz/¼ cup) pine nuts
30g (1oz/¼ cup) grated Parmesan
a large handful of basil
a handful of coriander (cilantro)
juice of ½ small lemon
4 tbsp olive oil
sea salt and freshly ground black pepper

Make the green tahini sauce: put the tahini, garlic, chilli, pine nuts, Parmesan, herbs and lemon juice in a food processor or blender and pulse to a thick, coarse paste. Add the olive oil and pulse again. Season to taste with salt and pepper.

Spiralise the courgettes using blade C (if you don't have a spiraliser, you can use a mandolin slicer or julienne peeler, but the 'noodles' will be thicker).

Cook the linguine in a large pan of salted boiling water according to the instructions on the packet.

While the pasta is cooking, lightly spray a griddle pan with olive oil and set over a medium heat. Add the tomatoes and cook for 4–6 minutes, turning occasionally, until softened and starting to char. Drizzle with the balsamic vinegar, remove and keep warm.

Meanwhile, dry-fry the halloumi in a large frying pan (skillet) for about 2 minutes each side until crisp and golden brown. Remove and keep warm.

Drain the cooked pasta, reserving 3–4 tablespoons of the cooking water, and mix with the spiralised courgettes (zucchini). Toss gently in the green tahini sauce, adding some of the reserved cooking water, if needed, to make a glossy sauce.

Stir in the griddled tomatoes and divide among four deep serving plates. Top with the halloumi and pine nuts, if using, and serve.

GRIDDLED HALLOUMI KEBABS

Halloumi is the only cheese that works really well in kebabs as it holds its shape and doesn't melt when cooked on a griddle, grill (broiler) or barbecue. Kebabs are so easy to assemble and make – you can even prepare them several hours in advance and leave them in the fridge to marinate until you're ready to cook.

SERVES 4
PREP 15 MINUTES
MARINATE 20–30 MINUTES
COOK 4–6 MINUTES

250g (9oz) halloumi, cubed
1 large aubergine (eggplant), cubed
2 red onions, cut into wedges
2 (bell) peppers, deseeded and cut into pieces
1 cucumber
warm flatbreads and tzatziki (see page 14), to serve

MARINADE
4 tbsp olive oil
juice of 1 lemon
2 garlic cloves, crushed
2 tbsp capers, diced
½ tsp paprika
a handful of basil, chopped
sea salt and freshly ground black pepper

Soak eight wooden skewers in some water for 20–30 minutes. This will prevent them burning when you cook the kebabs on the griddle pan.

Meanwhile, make the marinade: mix all the ingredients together in a bowl or blitz briefly in a food processor or blender.

Add the halloumi, aubergine (eggplant), onions and peppers and toss them gently in the marinade. Set aside for 20–30 minutes.

Thread the halloumi and vegetables alternately onto the skewers.

Heat a large ridged griddle pan over a medium to high heat. Add the kebabs to the hot pan and sear them for about 2–3 minutes each side until the vegetables are just tender and starting to char and the halloumi is golden brown.

Use a vegetable peeler to pare the cucumber lengthways into long thin strips.

Serve the kebabs with the cucumber strips, tzatziki and warm flatbreads.

VARIATIONS
- Add cherry tomatoes, button mushrooms or chunks of courgette (zucchini).
- Add peeled large prawns (jumbo shrimp).
- Substitute fresh mint or coriander (cilantro) for the basil.
- Swirl a little harissa into a bowl of chilled yoghurt to serve with the kebabs.

SESAME HALLOUMI WITH ROASTED VEGETABLES AND FIGS

//

Frying sliced halloumi in sesame seeds adds crunch and flavour to this dish. The combination of roasted vegetables and figs is surprisingly good, especially when they have a sticky sweet balsamic glaze and are tossed with bitter chicory leaves. To make this more substantial, serve it with roasted chicken, duck, pork or lamb.

SERVES 4
PREP 15 MINUTES
COOK 25 MINUTES

2 red onions, cut into thin wedges
1 red (bell) pepper, deseeded and cut into chunks
1 yellow (bell) pepper, deseeded and cut into chunks
olive oil, for drizzling
8 fresh figs, halved
3 tbsp balsamic vinegar
2 tsp brown sugar, e.g. Demerara
30g (1oz/¼ cup) chopped walnuts
250g (9oz) halloumi, cut into 8 slices
5 tbsp white sesame seeds
2 tbsp olive oil
2 large heads white or red chicory (Belgian endive), thickly sliced
sea salt and freshly ground black pepper
lemon wedges, to serve

Preheat the oven to 200°C (180°C fan)/400°F/gas 6.

Put the red onion and peppers in a large roasting pan and drizzle with olive oil. Roast in the oven for 10 minutes and then add the figs. Drizzle them with olive oil and sprinkle the balsamic vinegar and sugar over the top.

Return to the oven for 10 minutes and then add the walnuts. Roast for about 5 minutes until the figs and vegetables are tender and starting to get sticky and caramelised.

Meanwhile, press the halloumi into the sesame seeds to lightly coat both sides. Heat the olive oil in a large frying pan (skillet) set over a medium heat and fry the halloumi for 2–3 minutes each side until crisp and golden brown. Remove and drain on kitchen paper (paper towels).

Stir the chicory into the roasted figs and vegetables and season to taste. Divide among four serving plates and top with the sesame halloumi. Eat immediately before the halloumi cools down.

VARIATIONS
- Vary the vegetables for roasting – courgettes (zucchini), bulb fennel and aubergines (eggplants) all work well.
- Use torn radicchio leaves if you can't get chicory.

SALMON AND HALLOUMI POKE BOWL

//

You will need the best-quality salmon to make this Hawaiian-style poke bowl.
Buy the frozen sort and defrost in the fridge before using it.

SERVES 4
PREP 15 MINUTES
COOK 4 MINUTES

400g (14oz) wild salmon fillets,
   skinned and cubed
1 bunch of spring onions
   (scallions), thinly sliced
1 tbsp sesame oil
2 tbsp tamari or soy sauce
250g (9oz) halloumi
340g (12oz/scant 2 cups) cooked
   brown rice (still warm)
100g (4oz) wild rocket (arugula)
2 avocados, peeled, stoned
   and sliced
juice of 1 lime
a handful of coriander (cilantro),
   chopped
2 sheets nori, thinly sliced
Sriracha, for drizzling

Put the salmon in a bowl with the spring onions, sesame oil and tamari or soy sauce. Stir until the salmon and onions are well coated.

Cut the halloumi into fingers and dry-fry in a hot griddle pan set over a medium heat for 2–3 minutes each side until any liquid has been released and evaporated and the halloumi is golden brown and crispy on the outside and softened inside.

Mix the warm rice and rocket (arugula) together and divide among four shallow serving bowls. Add the salmon, avocado and halloumi. Sprinkle with lime juice and coriander and arrange the nori on top. Serve drizzled with Sriracha.

VARIATIONS
- Use sushi-grade tuna instead of salmon.
- Use a different hot sauce or sprinkle with chilli flakes.

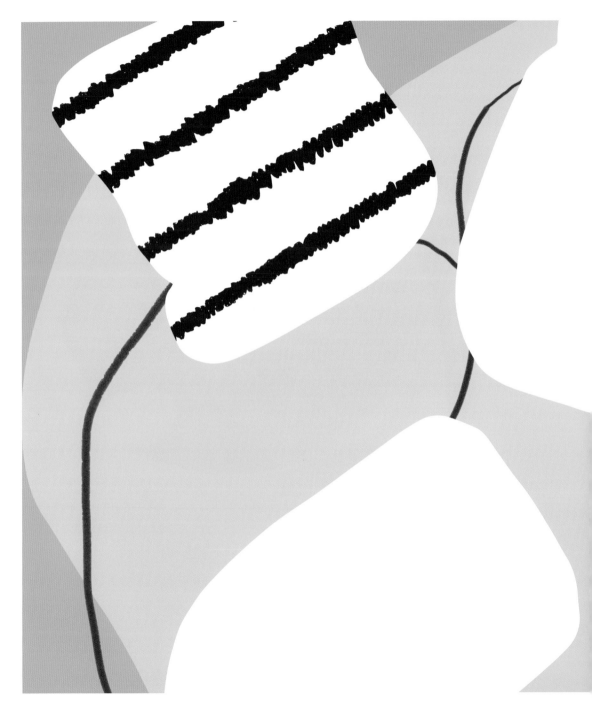

SALADS

WARM LENTIL, TOMATO AND HALLOUMI SALAD WITH PESTO

A great source of protein and fibre, lentils have an earthy flavour and fill you up. Don't be tempted to use the small red ones as they cook to a purée and don't retain their shape. This salad is best eaten lukewarm and it's especially good in winter when you tire of stodgy comfort food and fancy something lemony and refreshing.

SERVES 4
PREP 10 MINUTES
COOK 25–30 MINUTES

200g (7oz/generous 1 cup)
    Puy or green lentils
3 tbsp olive oil
1 onion, chopped
2 large carrots, finely diced
2 sticks celery, diced
2 garlic cloves, crushed
300g (10oz) baby plum
    tomatoes, halved
juice of 1 lemon
2 tbsp balsamic vinegar
a handful of basil, torn
200g (7oz) fine green beans,
    trimmed
250g (9oz) halloumi, cut into
    8 slices
2–3 tbsp green pesto,
    for drizzling
sea salt and freshly ground
    black pepper

Put the lentils in a saucepan and cover them with cold water. Bring to the boil, then reduce the heat and simmer gently for about 20 minutes until they are tender but still have a little bite. Drain and refresh under running cold water.

Meanwhile, heat 2 tablespoons olive oil in a large frying pan (skillet) and set over a low heat. Add the onion, carrots, celery and garlic and sweat them gently for 8–10 minutes, stirring occasionally, until softened.

Add the tomatoes and lentils and cook for 5 minutes, stirring occasionally. If the lentils start to stick, add a little water. Stir in the lemon juice, balsamic vinegar and basil and season to taste with salt and pepper. Remove from the heat and set aside to cool a little.

Cook the green beans in a pan of boiling water for 3–4 minutes until just tender but not too soft. Drain and refresh under running cold water.

Dry-fry or griddle the halloumi over a medium heat for about 2 minutes each side until crisp and golden brown.

Stir the remaining olive oil into the lentil mixture and divide among four serving plates. Top with the green beans and halloumi. Drizzle with pesto and eat immediately.

WINTER CHICORY, AVOCADO AND HALLOUMI SALAD

//

This crunchy salad of bitter chicory leaves, juicy apples, buttery avocado and fried halloumi is the perfect antidote to the winter blues. When it's cold and grey outside and you've tired of hearty soups, stews and carbs, this zingy salad will freshen your palate like a breath of fresh air.

SERVES 4
PREP 10 MINUTES
COOK 3–5 MINUTES

2 heads white or red chicory
    (Belgian endive)
1 bunch of spring onions
    (scallions), thinly sliced
1 ripe avocado, peeled, stoned
    and cubed
2 red apples, cored and cubed
85g (3oz/generous ½ cup)
    coarsely chopped walnuts
a bunch of flat-leaf parsley,
    finely chopped
olive oil, for brushing
250g (9oz) halloumi, cut into
    2cm (¾ inch) cubes
sea salt and freshly ground
    black pepper

HONEY MUSTARD DRESSING
4 tbsp fruity green olive oil
1 tbsp cider vinegar
juice of ½ lemon
2 tsp Dijon mustard
2 tsp runny honey

Make the honey mustard dressing: whisk all the ingredients together in a jug until smooth and well combined.

Trim the fat ends off the Belgian endives and slice the heads thinly into rounds.

Mix the chicory, spring onions (scallions), avocado, apples, walnuts and parsley in a bowl.

Lightly brush a large non-stick frying pan (skillet) with olive oil and set over a medium heat. When the pan is hot, add the halloumi and cook for about 2 minutes each side until crisp and golden brown all over.

Stir the halloumi into the chicory mixture and pour the dressing over the top. Toss gently and divide between four serving plates. Serve immediately while the halloumi is still warm.

VARIATIONS
- Use ripe pears instead of apples.
- Cubes of creamy blue cheese, e.g. Roquefort, make a good addition.
- Sprinkle the salad with pomegranate seeds.

HALLOUMI, RADICCHIO AND POMEGRANATE SALAD

Serve this colourful salad as a first course or as an accompaniment to roast chicken or lamb with quinoa, couscous or roast potatoes. The combination of red, white and green makes it a popular dish for Christmas.

SERVES 4
PREP 10 MINUTES
COOK 6–8 MINUTES

30g (1oz/scant ¼ cup) pine nuts
olive oil, for brushing
250g (9oz) halloumi, thinly sliced
1 head radicchio, separated
    into leaves
100g (4oz) baby spinach leaves
seeds of 1 pomegranate
1 tsp za'atar

DRESSING
4 tbsp olive oil
1 tbsp red wine vinegar
juice of ½ lemon
2 tbsp pomegranate molasses
1 tsp Dijon honey mustard

Heat a small frying pan (skillet) over a low to medium heat. Add the pine nuts and cook for 1–2 minutes, shaking the pan gently from time to time, until they are golden brown and release a nutty aroma. Remove immediately before they burn and set aside.

Make the dressing: whisk all the ingredients together until well combined.

Brush a ridged griddle pan with olive oil and set over a medium heat. When it's hot, add the halloumi and cook for 2 minutes each side until golden brown. Remove and keep warm.

Add some more olive oil to the pan with the radicchio and cook for about 2 minutes, turning occasionally, until warm and slightly golden brown around the edges.

Transfer to a bowl with the spinach, pomegranate seeds and toasted pine nuts. Toss gently in most of the dressing.

Divide among four serving plates and arrange the halloumi on top. Drizzle over the remaining dressing and sprinkle with za'atar. Serve immediately while the halloumi is hot.

GREEK SALAD WITH FRIED HALLOUMI

The traditional Greek salad is known as *horiatiki*, which comes from the word for country people or villagers. It's important to make it with only the best-quality and freshest ingredients, so don't be tempted to use inferior ones that are past their best. Use fragrant vine-ripened tomatoes and juicy Kalamata olives. Halloumi makes a delicious and interesting change from the usual salty feta.

SERVES 4
PREP 10 MINUTES
COOK 4 MINUTES

1 Greek or Lebanese cucumber,
  cut into chunks
4 large ripe tomatoes, cut
  into wedges
1 red onion, thinly sliced
16 large black olives, preferably
  Kalamata
a good pinch of dried Greek
  oregano
a pinch of sea salt crystals
250g (9oz) halloumi, sliced
90ml (3fl oz/⅓ cup) fruity
  green Greek olive oil
2 tbsp red wine vinegar
crusty bread, to serve

Mix together the cucumber, tomatoes, red onion and olives in a bowl. Sprinkle with the oregano and sea salt.

Set a large frying pan (skillet) over a medium to high heat and when it's hot, dry-fry the halloumi for about 2 minutes each side until crisp and golden brown.

Drizzle the olive oil and red wine vinegar over the salad and top with the hot halloumi. Serve immediately with crusty bread.

Tip: Greek and Lebanese cucumbers are quite small and very crunchy. If you can't get one, use a quarter of a regular long one.

VARIATIONS
· Add some chopped flat-leaf parsley, mint or capers.
· Mix in some thinly sliced fennel, green or red (bell) peppers and lamb's lettuce or rocket (arugula).
· It's not authentic but you can whisk the oil and vinegar together with a crushed garlic clove or lemon juice.

WARM BEAN, BACON AND HALLOUMI SALAD

Beans, bacon, avocado and halloumi are a winning combination of nutrients, textures and flavours. You don't have to use cannellini beans – canned butterbeans (lima beans), chickpeas (garbanzo beans), flageolet or haricot beans all work well.

SERVES 4
PREP 10 MINUTES
COOK 8–12 MINUTES

8 rashers (slices) streaky bacon
175g (6oz) halloumi, sliced
2 x 400g (14oz) cans cannellini
   beans, rinsed and drained
1 ripe avocado, peeled, stoned
   and cubed
100g (4oz) mixed rocket
   (arugula), baby spinach
   and watercress
freshly ground black pepper
lemon wedges, to serve

VINAIGRETTE
4 tbsp fruity green olive oil
juice of 1 lemon
1 tbsp balsamic vinegar
1 tsp runny honey
1 garlic clove, crushed
a few chives, snipped

Make the vinaigrette: whisk together all the ingredients in a bowl until well combined.

Set a large frying pan (skillet) over a medium to high heat and add the bacon to the hot pan. Cook for about 2–3 minutes each side until the bacon is golden brown and crisp. Remove and drain on kitchen paper (paper towels).

Add the halloumi to the pan and cook for about 2 minutes each side until crisp and golden brown. Remove and drain on kitchen paper.

Meanwhile, put the beans and a splash of water in a saucepan over a very low heat and heat gently for about 3–4 minutes until just lukewarm.

Put the beans in a bowl with the avocado and salad leaves. Pour over the vinaigrette and toss gently together.

Divide among four serving plates and add the halloumi. Crumble the crispy bacon over the top and serve with a good grinding of black pepper and lemon wedges for squeezing.

VIETNAMESE SALAD WITH FRIED HALLOUMI AND CASHEWS

///

If you've never considered topping an aromatic Vietnamese salad with halloumi, think again.
Its salty flavour and smooth texture are enhanced by the heat of the chilli and the pungent
nam pla (fish sauce). You can even eat it as a main course if you mix in some cooked rice noodles.

SERVES 4
PREP 15 MINUTES
COOK 7–8 MINUTES

85g (3oz/½ cup) unsalted
   cashews
250g (9oz) halloumi, sliced
2 large carrots, cut into thin
   matchsticks
2 courgettes (zucchini), cut
   into thin matchsticks
½ cucumber, cut into thin strips
4 spring onions (scallions),
   thinly sliced
a small handful of coriander
   (cilantro), chopped
a small handful of mint, chopped

DRESSING
2 tbsp peanut (groundnut) oil
1 tsp toasted sesame oil
1 tbsp nam pla (Thai fish sauce)
1 tbsp rice vinegar
juice of 1 lime
1 tbsp (soft) brown sugar
1 garlic clove, crushed
1 red bird's eye chilli, deseeded
   and diced

Make the dressing: mix all the ingredients together in a jug
or bowl until well combined.

Heat a large non-stick frying pan (skillet) over a medium heat.
Add the cashews and toss lightly for about 3 minutes until
golden brown and fragrant. Remove from the pan and set aside.

Add the halloumi to the pan and dry-fry for about 2 minutes
each side until crisp and golden brown. Remove.

Mix together the carrots, courgettes (zucchini), cucumber,
spring onions (scallions) and herbs. Toss gently in most of the
dressing and divide among four serving plates.

Arrange the halloumi on top and scatter with the toasted
cashews. Drizzle with the remaining dressing and serve
immediately.

VARIATIONS
• Use toasted peanuts instead of cashews.
• Add some diced ginger, soy sauce or toasted sesame
  seeds to the dressing.
• Mix some cherry tomatoes, bean sprouts, crisp lettuce
  leaves or shredded mangetout into the salad.
• Drizzle with sweet chilli sauce.

HALLOUMI PANZANELLA SALAD

//

This is a Greek version of the traditional Italian panzanella salad, which is made with stale bread. It's important to use a rustic country-style bread or, failing that, ciabatta. It's very filling and you could serve it as a main course with some grilled (broiled) chicken or fish.

SERVES 4
PREP 20 MINUTES
STAND 20–30 MINUTES
COOK 15 MINUTES

1 small red onion, thinly sliced
2 tbsp red wine vinegar
6 tbsp fruity green olive oil
2 ripe peaches, thickly sliced
8 thick slices of stale rustic bread
   or ciabatta
2 garlic cloves, peeled and halved
600g (1lb 5oz) vine-ripened juicy
   tomatoes, cut into chunks
175g (6oz) bottled charred (bell)
   peppers, cut into chunks
a handful of baby spinach leaves
a handful of flat-leaf parsley,
   coarsely shredded
a handful of basil, coarsely torn
250g (9oz) halloumi, thinly sliced

DRESSING
4 tbsp fruity green olive oil
2 tbsp red wine vinegar
1 garlic clove, crushed
a pinch of caster (superfine) sugar
sea salt and freshly ground
   black pepper

Put the red onion and vinegar in a bowl and set aside to marinate.

Make the dressing: whisk all the ingredients together in a jug.

Brush a ridged griddle pan with 1 tablespoon of the olive oil and set over a medium to high heat. Add the peaches and cook for about 2 minutes each side until starting to char. Remove and set aside.

Rub the slices of bread with the cut garlic cloves and drizzle them with the remaining olive oil. Cook on the hot griddle for 1–2 minutes each side until golden and slightly charred.

Roughly tear the bread into chunks and place them in a bowl with the peaches, marinated red onion, tomatoes, peppers, spinach leaves and herbs. Mix together well and toss gently in the dressing. Set aside for 20–30 minutes for the flavours to mingle.

When you're ready to serve, cook the halloumi, in batches, on a hot griddle pan for about 2 minutes each side until crisp, golden brown and attractively striped. Remove and drain on kitchen paper (paper towels).

Arrange the halloumi on top of the salad and serve immediately while it's hot.

WARM LEMONY SHRIMP AND HALLOUMI SALAD

Eat this salad with some couscous or pasta as a more substantial dish or just serve with fresh crusty bread to mop up the delicious warm garlicky dressing.

SERVES 4
PREP 10 MINUTES
COOK 12–16 MINUTES

4 tbsp pine nuts
2 tbsp olive oil
4 garlic cloves, crushed
a large handful of flat-leaf
    parsley, chopped
a large handful of basil, chopped
5 tbsp ouzo or white vermouth,
    e.g. Noilly Prat
juice of 1 large lemon
600g (1lb 5oz) shelled large raw
    prawns (jumbo shrimp)
250g (9oz) halloumi, cut into
    2cm (¾ inch) cubes
a pinch of cayenne or paprika
torn leaves of 1 large or 2 small
    radicchios
sea salt and freshly ground
    black pepper

Heat a small frying pan (skillet) over a low to medium heat. Add the pine nuts and cook for 1–2 minutes, shaking the pan gently from time to time, until they are golden brown and release a nutty aroma. Remove immediately before they burn and set aside.

Heat the olive oil in a large frying pan (skillet) set over a medium heat. Add the garlic and cook for 1 minute until softened but not coloured. Stir in a little of the parsley and basil and then add the ouzo or vermouth. Turn up the heat and let it reduce a little, then add the lemon juice and the remaining herbs. Cook gently over a low heat for 3–4 minutes.

Add the prawns to the pan and cook for 1–2 minutes each side until they turn pink. Take the pan off the heat and season to taste with salt and pepper.

Dry-fry the halloumi in a non-stick frying pan (skillet) over a medium heat for about 2 minutes each side, until golden brown and crispy on the outside and softened inside. Remove from the pan and dust with cayenne or paprika.

Divide the radicchio among four serving plates. Spoon the prawns and the pan juices over the top. Scatter with the halloumi and pine nuts and serve immediately.

VARIATION
• Omit the prawns and cook some cubed chicken breast in the olive oil until golden brown all over, before adding the herbs, alcohol and lemon juice. Cook gently for about 10 minutes or so until the chicken is cooked through and the liquid has reduced.

BAKED AUBERGINE (EGGPLANT) SALAD WITH HALLOUMI AND MINT

The smoky, mild tenderness of baked aubergine (eggplant) is the perfect partner for griddled halloumi and it features in many Levantine salads and meze. The cooling yoghurt and tahini dressing complements the salty cheese and spicy harissa.

SERVES 4
PREP 15 MINUTES
COOK 20 MINUTES

2 aubergines (eggplants),
   trimmed
3 tbsp olive oil, plus extra
   for brushing
2 tsp harissa
3 tbsp pine nuts
250g (9oz) halloumi, cut into
   fingers
75g (3oz) wild rocket (arugula)
a handful of mint, finely chopped
balsamic vinegar, for drizzling
seeds of ½ pomegranate
warm pitta bread, to serve

YOGHURT AND TAHINI
   DRESSING
120g (4½oz/½ cup) natural
   yoghurt
1 tbsp tahini
2 garlic cloves, crushed
1 tbsp olive oil
grated zest and juice of ½ lemon
sea salt and freshly ground
   black pepper

Preheat the oven to 190°C (170°C fan)/375°F/gas 5.

Make the yoghurt and tahini dressing: mix all the ingredients together in a bowl. Season to taste with salt and pepper and set aside.

Cut the aubergines (eggplants) into thin slices lengthways. Mix the olive oil and harissa together and brush over both sides of the aubergines (eggplant). Place on a baking tray (cookie sheet) and bake in the oven for about 20 minutes until golden brown.

Meanwhile, set a small frying pan (skillet) over a medium heat. When it's hot, add the pine nuts and toast for 1–2 minutes, tossing them gently until they are golden brown and release their nutty fragrance. Remove from the pan immediately before they burn.

Lightly oil a griddle pan and place over a high heat. Add the halloumi and cook for about 2 minutes each side until crisp and golden brown all over.

Put the baked aubergines (eggplant) in a large bowl with the rocket (arugula) and mint. Lightly toss everything together and drizzle the yoghurt and tahini dressing over the top. Add the hot halloumi and sprinkle with the balsamic vinegar, toasted pine nuts and pomegranate seeds. Serve immediately with warm triangles of pitta bread – you can toast them or heat them on the oiled griddle pan.

HALLOUMI AND HUMMUS SALAD WITH PITTA CHIPS

//

These golden-brown crispy pitta chips are really spicy and delicious.
They will stay fresh and crisp for up to 3 days if stored in an airtight container.

SERVES 4
PREP 20 MINUTES
COOK 12–14 MINUTES

250g (9oz) halloumi, sliced
3 ripe tomatoes, cut into wedges
½ red onion, thinly sliced
1 green or red (bell) pepper,
  deseeded and sliced
2 tbsp fruity green olive oil
1 tbsp red wine vinegar

PITTA CHIPS
4 pitta breads
olive oil, for brushing
a pinch of dried chilli flakes
a pinch of sea salt

HUMMUS
2 x 400g (14oz) cans chickpeas
  (garbanzo beans)
3 garlic cloves, crushed
100g (4oz/scant ½ cup) of tahini
2 tsp ground cumin
3 tbsp olive oil, plus extra
  for drizzling
juice of 1 lemon, plus extra
  for drizzling
a pinch of sea salt crystals
chopped parsley, for sprinkling
za'atar, paprika or sumac,
  for dusting

Preheat the oven to 180°C (160°C fan)/350°F/gas 4.

Slice each pitta bread in half so you have two large thin pieces
of bread. Cut each slice into strips and lightly brush with olive oil.
Arrange them on a lightly oiled baking tray (cookie sheet) and
sprinkle with the chilli flakes and sea salt.

Bake in the oven for about 10 minutes until crisp and golden.
Remove and set aside to cool on a wire rack.

Make the hummus: rinse and drain the chickpeas (garbanzo
beans) then blitz them with the garlic, tahini, cumin, olive oil
and lemon juice in a blender or food processor until you have a
coarse purée. If it's too thick, thin it down with a little water or
some liquid from the canned chickpeas. Season to taste with salt
and transfer to a bowl. Sprinkle with parsley, dust with spices and
drizzle with olive oil and lemon juice.

Dry-fry the halloumi in a non-stick frying pan (skillet) over
a medium heat for about 2 minutes each side until golden brown
and crispy on the outside and softened inside.

Smear the hummus in a circle around the edge of four serving
plates, leaving a well in the centre. Mix together the tomatoes,
onion and pepper in a bowl and toss in the olive oil and vinegar.
Spoon into the centre of each plate and top with the hot
halloumi. Serve immediately with the pitta chips.

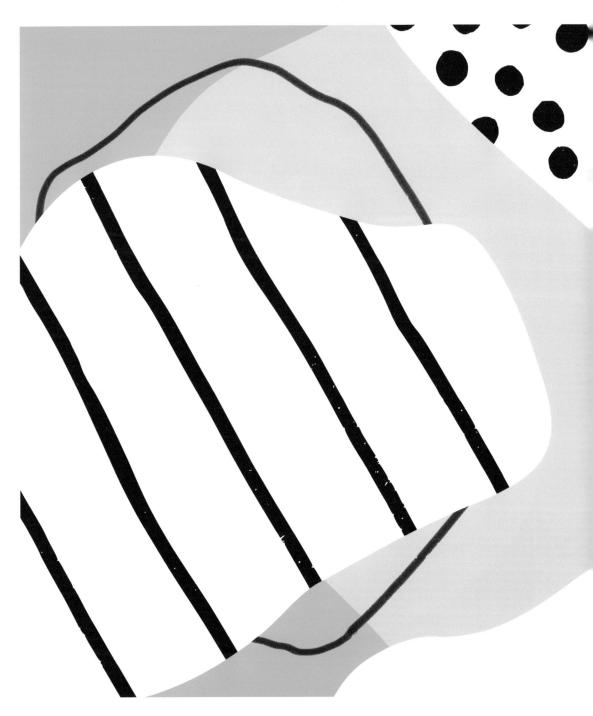

DINNERS

HALLOUMI AND SWEET POTATO BURGERS

///

If you don't want to fry the burgers, you can cook them on a lightly oiled griddle
pan or bake them in the oven. They can also be served in warmed pitta bread.

SERVES 4
PREP 20 MINUTES
CHILL 30 MINUTES
COOK 25 MINUTES

500g (1lb 2oz) sweet potatoes,
    peeled and cubed
175g (6oz) kale, shredded
1 tbsp olive oil, plus extra
    for frying
8 spring onions (scallions),
    finely chopped
2 garlic cloves, crushed
1 red chilli, deseeded and diced
a handful of coriander (cilantro),
    chopped
2 tbsp plain (all-purpose) flour
50g (2oz/generous ¼ cup)
    sesame seeds
250g (9oz) halloumi, sliced
4 wholegrain burger buns
1 ripe avocado, peeled, stoned
    and mashed
sea salt and freshly ground
    black pepper
chilli jam, to serve

Cook the sweet potatoes in a large pan of boiling salted water
for about 15 minutes until just tender. Drain and cool before
roughly crushing with a potato masher – don't mash to a purée.

Meanwhile, cook the kale in a pan of boiling water for about
4 minutes until just tender. Drain and dry with kitchen paper.
Cool, then chop it coarsely.

Heat the olive oil in a small frying pan (skillet) set over a medium
heat and cook the spring onions (scallions), garlic and chilli for
2–3 minutes without colouring. Stir in the coriander (cilantro).

Spoon into a large bowl, then mix in the sweet potato, kale and
flour. Season with salt and pepper. Divide the mixture into four
portions and shape each one into a burger. Coat in the sesame
seeds, then cover and chill in the fridge for 30 minutes until firm.

Heat a little oil in a non-stick frying pan (skillet) over a low to
medium heat and cook the burgers for 3–4 minutes each side until
golden brown. Remove and drain on kitchen paper (paper towels).

Dry-fry or griddle the halloumi over a medium heat for about
2 minutes each side until crisp and golden brown.

Lightly toast the burger buns and spread the bases with the
mashed avocado. Top with the halloumi, burgers and some chilli
jam. Cover with the bun tops and serve.

> Tip: If the burger mixture seems a bit soft and loose, stir in
> a little more flour to bind it.

SEEDY HALLOUMI AND ROASTED VEGETABLE TRAYBAKE

A traybake is so easy to make – you just cook everything in one pan and there's hardly any washing up afterwards. Loaded with seeds and vegetables, this makes a really healthy supper. Vegetarians can omit the Parma ham.

SERVES 4
PREP 15 MINUTES
COOK 30–35 MINUTES

2 red onions, cut into wedges
1 red (bell) pepper, deseeded and cut into chunks
1 yellow (bell) pepper, deseeded and cut into chunks
400g (14oz) sweet potato, peeled and cut into chunks
3 large carrots, cut into chunky matchsticks
4 tbsp olive oil
1 tsp crushed coriander seeds
50g (2oz/scant ½ cup) sunflower or flax seeds
250g (9oz) halloumi, cut into 2cm (¾ inch) cubes
8 wafer-thin slices of lean Parma ham
200g (7oz) baby spinach leaves
good-quality balsamic vinegar, for drizzling
1 tbsp black sesame seeds
sea salt and freshly ground black pepper

Preheat the oven to 190°C (170°C fan)/375°F/gas 5.

Put the red onions, peppers, sweet potato and carrots in a large roasting pan. Drizzle with the olive oil and sprinkle the coriander seeds over the top. Season lightly with salt and pepper, and toss everything together gently.

Roast in the oven for 20–25 minutes until the vegetables are just tender. Stir in the sunflower or flax seeds and scatter the halloumi over the top. Return to the oven and cook for a further 10 minutes until the halloumi is golden brown.

Meanwhile, dry-fry the Parma ham for 1–2 minutes in a large frying pan (skillet) set over a medium heat. When it's really crisp and golden brown, remove and drain on kitchen paper (paper towels).

Stir the spinach into the hot vegetable and cheese mixture – it will wilt but retain its lovely fresh green colour.

Divide among four serving plates and top with the crispy Parma ham. Drizzle with balsamic vinegar and sprinkle with the black sesame seeds.

VARIATIONS
- Add some chunks of aubergine (eggplant) or courgette (zucchini).
- For a more spicy flavour, add some cumin seeds or chilli flakes.
- Drizzle with green pesto.

SICILIAN-STUFFED PEPPERS WITH ROASTED HALLOUMI

//

This healthy Mediterranean dish is equally good eaten warm from the oven or cold the following day. The orange juice and sultanas add a sweet fruitiness. If you like the Sicilian agrodolce (sweet-and-sour) flavouring, you can drizzle the cooked peppers with some good-quality syrupy balsamic vinegar just before serving.

SERVES 4
PREP 10 MINUTES
COOK 45 MINUTES

4 red or yellow (bell) peppers
olive oil, for brushing
juice of 2 oranges
250g (9oz) halloumi, cut into
   8 slices
salad, to serve

STUFFING
60ml (2fl oz/¼ cup) extra-virgin
   olive oil
1 onion, finely chopped
3 garlic cloves, crushed
100g (4oz/generous ½ cup)
   pine nuts
250g (9oz/3 cups) fresh white
   breadcrumbs
100g/4oz (¾ cup) sultanas
   (golden raisins)
2 tbsp capers
a handful of flat-leaf parsley,
   chopped
4 anchovy fillets in oil, diced
   (optional)
grated zest and juice of 1 lemon
sea salt and freshly ground black
   pepper

Preheat the oven to 180°C (160°C fan)/350°F/gas 4.

Make the stuffing: heat the oil in a large frying pan (skillet) set over a low heat. Add the onion and garlic and cook, stirring occasionally, for 8–10 minutes until softened. Stir in the pine nuts and breadcrumbs and cook for 2–3 minutes.

Remove from the heat and stir in the sultanas, capers, parsley and anchovies (if using). Mix in the lemon zest and juice and season to taste with salt and pepper. If the mixture seems a little dry, add some more olive oil to moisten it.

Cut the peppers lengthways through the stalk into two halves. Remove the white ribs and seeds. Fill them with the stuffing mixture and place in a large roasting pan that has been lightly oiled.

Bake in the oven for about 30 minutes until the peppers are cooked and tender and starting to char around the edges.

Pour the orange juice over the peppers and place a slice of halloumi on top of each one.

Pop under a hot grill (broiler) for 3–5 minutes until the halloumi is golden brown. Serve immediately with salad.

HALLOUMI AND SPINACH TART

//

This is a delicious variation on the traditional Greek *spanakopita* (spinach pie), which is made with feta cheese and filo (phyllo) pastry. It's easy to make if you use ready-rolled puff pastry.

SERVES 4

PREP 15 MINUTES

COOK 40 MINUTES

2 tbsp olive oil, plus extra
    for greasing
2 onions, finely chopped
2 garlic cloves, crushed
400g (14oz) spinach, trimmed
juice of ½ lemon
a handful of dill, chopped
a pinch of nutmeg
200g (7oz) halloumi, grated
425g (14oz) pack ready-rolled
    puff pastry sheets (2 sheets)
1 medium free-range egg, beaten
sea salt and freshly ground
    black pepper

Preheat the oven to 200°C (180°C fan)/400°F/gas 6.

Heat the olive oil in a frying pan (skillet) set over a medium heat and cook the onions and garlic for 6–8 minutes until tender. Stir in the spinach and cook for 1–2 minutes until it wilts.

Transfer to a bowl and stir in the lemon juice, dill, nutmeg and grated halloumi. Season to taste with salt and pepper.

Lightly oil a baking tray (cookie sheet) and place one of the puff pastry sheets on it. Brush around the edge with beaten egg. Spread out the remaining sheet and use to cut out a 2cm (¾ inch) wide border (like the frame around a painting). Lay it on top of the other pastry sheet and prick the base inside the border with a fork.

Bake in the oven for about 10 minutes until the pastry is slightly risen and golden brown. Remove from the oven and fill the centre with the spinach and halloumi mixture. Cut the remaining puff pastry into strips about 2cm (¾ inches) wide and arrange them in a criss-cross lattice over the top of the filling. Brush all the pastry lightly with beaten egg.

Bake in the oven for about 20 minutes until the pastry is puffy, crisp and golden brown. Serve hot, cut into slices.

HALLOUMI MAC 'N' CHEESE

//

This deluxe version of a traditional macaroni cheese delivers a good portion of your recommended 5-a-day vegetables. If you can't find any Kefalotyri (a hard Greek cheese), use grated mature Cheddar or even Parmesan instead.

SERVES 4
PREP 15 MINUTES
COOK 35–40 MINUTES

200g (7oz/2 cups) macaroni (dry weight)
2 tbsp olive oil
2 large leeks, trimmed and sliced
300g (10oz) button mushrooms, quartered
20 baby plum tomatoes, halved
a handful of flat-leaf parsley, chopped
2 tbsp grated halloumi
2 tbsp grated Kefalotyri
4 tbsp fresh white or wholemeal breadcrumbs

WHITE SAUCE
50g (2oz/¼ cup) butter
50g (2oz/½ cup) plain (all-purpose) flour
600ml (1 pint/2½ cups) milk
a pinch of ground nutmeg
100g (4oz/¾ cup) grated halloumi
100g (4oz/¾ cup) grated Kefalotyri
sea salt and freshly ground black pepper

Preheat the oven to 190°C (170° fan)/375°F/gas 5.

Cook the macaroni in a large pan of lightly salted boiling water according to the packet instructions. Drain and keep warm.

Meanwhile, heat the olive oil in a frying pan (skillet) set over a low to medium heat. Add the leeks and mushrooms and cook gently for 5 minutes until softened. Stir in the tomatoes and parsley and cook for 2 minutes.

Make the white sauce: melt the butter in a saucepan over a low heat and stir in the flour with a wooden spoon until you have a thick paste. Cook for 2 minutes without browning and then start adding the milk, a little at a time, beating well with a balloon whisk between each addition until smooth and free of lumps.

Cook gently, whisking or stirring all the time, for about 5 minutes until the sauce is thick and smooth and coats the back of the spoon. Stir in the nutmeg and grated cheeses, and season to taste with salt and pepper. Stir in the macaroni.

Spread half the macaroni in the base of an ovenproof dish and spoon the vegetables over the top. Cover with the remaining macaroni and sprinkle with the grated cheeses and breadcrumbs.

Bake in the oven for about 20 minutes, until bubbling, crisp and golden brown.

SPICY SWEET POTATO HALLOUMI TRIANGLES

Serve these crisp, golden filo parcels for supper or as a party snack or canapé. You can prepare them in advance and cook them when you're ready to eat. They also reheat successfully in a medium oven.

SERVES 4
PREP 30 MINUTES
COOK 35 MINUTES

12 sheets of filo (phyllo) pastry
olive oil, for brushing
smashed beans or chickpeas
    (garbanzo beans) and salad,
    to serve

SPICY SWEET POTATO FILLING
500g (1lb 2oz) sweet potatoes,
    peeled and cubed
1 tbsp olive oil
4 spring onions (scallions),
    finely chopped
2 garlic cloves, crushed
1 red chilli, diced
1 tsp cumin seeds
1 tsp fennel seeds
200g (7oz) baby spinach leaves
grated zest of 1 lemon
a handful of chopped coriander
    (cilantro)
250g (9oz) halloumi, cut into
    1cm (½ inch) cubes
sea salt and freshly ground
    black pepper

Preheat the oven to 200°C (180°C fan)/400°F/gas 6.

Make the spicy sweet potato filling: cook the sweet potato in a pan of boiling water for about 10 minutes until just tender – don't overcook so it's too soft and mushy. Drain well.

Meanwhile, heat the olive oil in a pan set over a low heat and cook the spring onions (scallions), garlic and chilli for 2–3 minutes until softened. Add the seeds and cook for 1 minute. Stir in the spinach, lemon zest and coriander and cook for 1 minute until the spinach wilts. Stir in the halloumi and sweet potato and remove from the heat. Season to taste with salt and pepper.

Place one sheet of filo pastry on a clean worktop and brush lightly with oil. Cover with another sheet and brush with oil. Cut lengthways down the middle into two long rectangles.

Put a spoonful of the filling into the top right-hand corner of each strip of pastry. Fold the pastry over the filling at an angle to make a triangle, then keep on folding it over until you get to the bottom of the strip and have a neat triangular parcel. Repeat with the remaining filo pastry and filling mixture until you have 12 parcels.

Brush the filo parcels lightly with oil and place on a baking tray (cookie sheet) lined with baking parchment. Cook in the oven for 25 minutes until crisp and golden. Serve with smashed beans or chickpeas (garbanzo beans) and salad.

HALLOUMI AND AUBERGINE (EGGPLANT) PIZZA

//

This Levantine-style pizza is flavoured with caramelised onions, warm Middle Eastern spices, resinous pine nuts and sweet sultanas. If you're in a hurry, use ready-made pizza bases or large flatbreads.

MAKES 4 PIZZAS
PREP 30 MINUTES
RISE 1–2 HOURS
COOK 35 MINUTES

500g (1lb 2oz/4 cups) strong
   plain flour, plus extra for
   dusting
7g (¼ oz) sachet fast-action
   dried yeast
1 tsp sea salt
300ml (11fl oz/1¼ cups)
   warm water

HALLOUMI AND AUBERGINE
   (EGGPLANT) TOPPING
2 medium aubergines (eggplants),
   trimmed and cut into rounds
3 tbsp olive oil, plus extra
   for drizzling
3 onions, thinly sliced
4 tbsp pine nuts
85g (3oz/generous ½ cup)
   sultanas (golden raisins)
½ tsp cumin seeds
a pinch of cayenne pepper
250g (9oz) halloumi, grated
sea salt and freshly ground
   black pepper

Put the flour, yeast and salt in a large mixing bowl. Make a well in the centre and pour in most of the warm water. Mix to a soft dough, drawing in the flour from the sides with your hand. Alternatively, use an electric mixer fitted with a dough hook attachment. If the dough is too dry, add some more warm water.

Knead the ball of dough on a floured work surface for 10 minutes until smooth and elastic (or use the electric mixer). Place in a large lightly oiled bowl and cover with a clean damp cloth. Leave in a warm place for 1–2 hours until well risen and doubled in size.

Meanwhile, make the topping: drizzle some oil over the aubergine (eggplant) slices and cook, in batches, in a ridged griddle pan set over a medium heat for 2–3 minutes each side until golden brown. Remove and drain on kitchen paper (paper towels).

Heat the olive oil in a large frying pan (skillet) set over a low heat. Add the onions and cook, stirring occasionally, for about 20 minutes until really soft and starting to caramelise. Remove from the heat and stir in the pine nuts and sultanas (golden raisins). Season with salt and pepper and add the cumin seeds and cayenne.

Preheat the oven to 230°C (210°C fan)/450°F/gas 8.

Knock the dough down with your fist and knead it lightly on a floured work surface. Cut into four equal-sized pieces and roll each thinly into a large circle. Place on four baking trays (cookie sheets).

Spoon the onion mixture over the pizza bases, leaving a 2.5cm (1 inch) border around the edge for the crust to rise. Top with the griddled aubergines (eggplant) and grated halloumi, then drizzle with olive oil.

Bake the pizzas in the oven for about 12–15 minutes until the pizza bases are crisp and golden brown. Serve immediately.

LEMONY HALLOUMI PASTA

///

The grated halloumi combines well with the creamy lemony sauce. Don't add salt unless you feel it needs some at the very end just before serving – the halloumi will provide it naturally. You can enhance the flavour and make it more robust by adding a dash of lemon juice or some crushed garlic, if wished.

SERVES 4
PREP 10 MINUTES
COOK 10 MINUTES

50g (2oz/⅓ cup) pine nuts
400g (14oz) linguine (dried weight)
1 vegetable stock cube
225g (8oz/1½ cups) shelled peas
250g (9oz) asparagus, trimmed and cut into 2.5cm (1 inch) lengths
200g (7oz/generous ¾ cup) half-fat crème fraîche
grated zest of 1 lemon
100g (4oz) baby spinach leaves
100g (4oz/¾ cup) grated halloumi
a handful of flat-leaf parsley, chopped
freshly ground black pepper

Heat a small frying pan (skillet) over a low to medium heat. Add the pine nuts and cook for 1–2 minutes, shaking the pan gently from time to time, until they are golden brown and release a nutty aroma. Remove immediately before they burn and set aside.

Cook the pasta in a large pan of boiling water, to which you've added a vegetable stock cube, according to the instructions on the packet. Add the peas and asparagus for the last 4–5 minutes of the cooking time.

Meanwhile, heat the crème fraîche and lemon zest in a small saucepan set over a low heat.

Drain the pasta and vegetables, reserving 2–3 tablespoons of the cooking liquid, and return to the hot pan. Stir in the warm crème fraîche and spinach leaves and let them wilt into the pasta. Add the reserved cooking liquid to thin the sauce, if needed.

Stir in most of the halloumi and parsley, season with black pepper and divide among four shallow serving bowls. Sprinkle with the remaining halloumi and toasted pine nuts and serve.

LOADED HALLOUMI FLATBREADS

//

These loaded flatbreads are surprisingly filling, but you can add griddled chicken or lamb, roasted vegetables or whatever takes your fancy.

SERVES 4
PREP 20 MINUTES
COOK 10 MINUTES

250g (9oz) halloumi, cut
   into 12 fingers
4 large flatbreads or wraps
125g (4½oz) hummus
1 tbsp harissa

CRUNCHY SALAD

½ small red cabbage, shredded
2 carrots, coarsely grated
1 small red onion, grated
4 medjool dates, stoned
   (pitted) and chopped
1 x 400g (14oz) can chickpeas
   (garbanzo beans), rinsed
   and drained
a handful of coriander
   (cilantro), chopped
juice of 1 orange

DRESSING

2 tbsp olive oil
1 red chilli, diced
1 tsp grated fresh root ginger
1 tsp cumin seeds
1 tsp black mustard seeds
200g (7oz/¾ cup) Greek yoghurt
sea salt and freshly ground
   black pepper

Make the crunchy salad: mix all the ingredients together in a bowl.

Make the dressing: heat the oil in a small frying pan (skillet) over a low heat. Add the chilli and ginger and cook for 2 minutes, then stir in the seeds. Cook for 1–2 minutes until fragrant. Put the yoghurt in a clean bowl and stir in the chilli, ginger and seed mixture. Season to taste. Gently toss the salad in the dressing.

Dry-fry the halloumi in a non-stick frying pan (skillet) over a medium heat for 2–3 minutes each side until golden brown and crispy on the outside and softened inside. Remove and drain on kitchen paper (paper towels).

Warm the flatbreads on a griddle pan or in a low oven and spread them with the hummus. Top with the halloumi and crunchy salad, and dot with harissa. Serve immediately.

HONEY-BAKED CHICKEN WITH HALLOUMI

This simple dish is so delicious and easy to make – perfect for supper after a busy day. If you don't have foraged wild greens, don't worry. You can use baby spinach leaves, rocket (arugula), chard, spring greens or whatever you can find in your local supermarket or greengrocers.

SERVES 4
PREP 10 MINUTES
COOK 25 MINUTES

600g (1lb 5oz) skinless chicken breast fillets
leaves stripped from a few sprigs of lemon thyme
2 tbsp runny honey, preferably Greek thyme honey
2 tbsp fruity green olive oil
1 garlic clove, crushed
finely pared zest and juice of 1 lemon
250g (9oz) halloumi, cut into 8 slices
sea salt and freshly ground black pepper
roast or baked potatoes, to serve
lemon wedges, to serve

WILD GREENS
800g (1lb 12oz) wild greens, e.g. dandelion leaves, spinach, rocket (arugula), chard or beetroot (beet) leaves, washed and stalks trimmed
5 tbsp fruity green olive oil
3 tbsp lemon juice

Preheat the oven to 180°C (160°C fan)/350°F/gas 4.

Put the chicken and thyme leaves in a large roasting pan. Mix together the honey, olive oil, garlic and lemon zest and juice and sprinkle over the top, turning the chicken to coat it all over. Season with a pinch of salt and some freshly ground black pepper.

Bake in the oven for 15 minutes, then add the halloumi and bake for 10 minutes until golden brown and the chicken is cooked through.

Meanwhile, make the wild greens: blanch the leaves in a large pan of boiling salted water. The chard and beetroot leaves will need 4–5 minutes, whereas the dandelion, spinach and rocket (arugula) will wilt in 2 minutes. They should be just tender and retain their lovely fresh green colour. Drain well.

Blend the olive oil and lemon juice to make a dressing and toss the leaves in it. Season lightly with salt and pepper.

Serve the chicken and halloumi with the wild greens, some roast or baked potatoes and lemon wedges.

LAMB AND HALLOUMI KEBABS WITH ORZO

Orzo is becoming increasingly popular and you can now buy it in most delis and supermarkets as well as online. Although it looks like large grains of rice, it's actually a type of pasta. It's often served in Greece with meat kebabs and stews.

SERVES 4
PREP 20 MINUTES
MARINATE 30 MINUTES
COOK 12 MINUTES

450g (1lb) boneless lean leg
    of lamb, cut into 2cm
    (¾ inch) cubes
250g (9oz) halloumi, cut into
    2cm (¾ inch) cubes
225g (8oz/generous 1 cup) orzo
    (dried weight)
1 red onion, cut into wedges
4 spring onions (scallions),
    finely chopped
a handful of flat-leaf parsley,
    finely chopped
2 tbsp olive oil
juice of 1 lemon
sea salt and freshly ground
    black pepper
hot chilli sauce and tzatziki (see
    page 14), to serve (optional)

MARINADE
2 tbsp olive oil
grated zest and juice of 1 lemon
2 garlic cloves, crushed
a pinch of crushed chilli flakes
2 tbsp dried oregano

To make the marinade: whisk all the ingredients together in a large bowl.

Add the lamb and halloumi and stir well until they are coated all over in the marinade. Cover the bowl and leave to marinate in the fridge for at least 30 minutes.

Cook the orzo according to the instructions on the packet.

Thread the lamb, halloumi and red onions onto four long metal skewers, lightly brushing them with any leftover marinade.

Cook under a preheated grill (broiler) or on a hot barbecue for about 12 minutes, turning occasionally, until they are browned all over. The lamb should still be a little pink in the middle.

Drain the orzo and return to the warm pan. Stir in the spring onions (scallions), parsley, olive oil and lemon juice and season to taste with salt and pepper.

Serve the kebabs immediately with the warm orzo and some hot chilli sauce or cooling tzatziki, if wished.

CHICKEN SOUVLAKI WITH HALLOUMI

//

This is quintessentially Greek fast street food – griddled chicken and halloumi wrapped in a pitta sandwich. It's really healthy and delicious. For a more smoky, charred flavour, you can cook the skewers over hot coals on a barbecue. Alternatively, serve the skewers with the salad vegetables, drizzled with tzatziki, on a plate with the warm pitta breads on the side.

SERVES 4
PREP 10 MINUTES
MARINATE 30 MINUTES
COOK 10–12 MINUTES

4 skinless boneless chicken
   breasts, cut into 2cm
   (¾ inch) cubes
250g (9oz) halloumi, cut into
   2cm (¾ inch) cubes
8 pitta breads
a few cos (romaine) lettuce leaves
2 juicy tomatoes, cut into large
   chunks
½ red onion, thinly sliced
120g (4oz/½ cup) Tzatziki (see
   page 14)
fried potato chips (French fries),
   to serve (optional)
lemon wedges, to serve

MARINADE
4 tbsp fruity green olive oil
juice of 1 lemon
2 garlic cloves, crushed
1 tbsp dried oregano
sea salt and freshly ground
   black pepper

Make the marinade: whisk all the ingredients together in a large bowl.

Add the chicken cubes and stir well until they are coated all over in the marinade. Cover the bowl and leave to marinate in the fridge for at least 30 minutes.

Meanwhile, soak 8 wooden skewers in some water for about 20–30 minutes. This will prevent them burning when you cook the kebabs in the griddle pan.

Thread the chicken and halloumi onto the skewers, lightly brushing the halloumi with any leftover marinade.

Set a large griddle pan over a medium to high heat. Cook the skewers for about 10–12 minutes, turning them occasionally, until golden brown all over and the chicken is thoroughly cooked.

Warm the pitta breads in the griddle pan or a low oven.

To eat the souvlaki in the traditional way, remove the chicken and halloumi from the skewers and mix with the lettuce, tomatoes and red onion in a bowl. Divide among the pitta breads and drizzle with the tzatziki. Fold the pitta bread around the filling and then wrap in some kitchen foil or baking parchment, tucking in the end to hold the pitta in place. This makes it easier to eat it in your hands. You can add fried chunky potato chips to the souvlaki filling, if wished. Serve with lemon wedges to squeeze over the top.

GRILLED SARDINES WITH HALLOUMI AND STICKY FIGS

///

This dish might seem a bit fiddly, but it's really easy to make and you can prepare the four-seed crust in advance. You need to use the best and freshest sardines you can find for the best results. Ask the fishmonger to scale and gut them for you if you're squeamish.

SERVES 4
PREP 15 MINUTES
COOK 10–15 MINUTES

12 sardines, scaled and gutted
grated zest and juice of 1 lemon
½ tsp crushed chilli flakes
olive oil, for drizzling
a few sprigs of mint, chopped
a few sprigs of coriander
    (cilantro), chopped
sea salt and freshly ground
    black pepper
lemon wedges, to serve

STICKY FIGS

4 tsp olive oil
2 tsp balsamic vinegar
8 large fresh figs, halved
pomegranate molasses,
    for drizzling

**FOUR-SEED CRUSTED
    HALLOUMI**

1 tsp cumin seeds
1 tsp fenugreek seeds
1 tsp nigella seeds
1 tsp fennel seeds
250g (9oz) halloumi,
    cut into 12 fingers
2 tsp olive oil

Preheat the grill (broiler) to high. Season the sardines with salt and pepper and place in a grill (broiler) pan lined with kitchen foil. Sprinkle them with the lemon zest and chilli flakes and drizzle over some olive oil. Grill for about 2 minutes each side until golden brown and cooked through. Sprinkle with the lemon juice and keep warm.

Make the sticky figs: whisk the olive oil and balsamic vinegar in a large bowl. Add the figs and turn them gently to coat them all over. Heat a ridged griddle pan over a medium to high heat and cook the figs for 2–3 minutes each side until slightly browned and striped. Remove and drizzle with the pomegranate molasses.

Meanwhile, make the four-seed crusted halloumi: put the seeds in a pestle and mortar and crush lightly together. Don't pulverise them to a powder. Press the halloumi into this seedy mixture. Heat the olive oil in a frying pan (skillet) over a medium heat and fry the halloumi for about 2 minutes each side until golden brown and crusty.

Serve the sardines with the halloumi and sticky figs, sprinkled with mint and coriander (cilantro), with lemon wedges for squeezing. Boiled potatoes go well with this.

Tip: You can cook the sardines in a hot griddle pan, if you prefer.

CHORIZO, PRAWN AND HALLOUMI SKEWERS

//

This surf-and-turf combo works really well with halloumi. We've cooked the skewers on a griddle pan, but you could use a hot barbecue for a really smoky flavour. They also make great party canapés, turned into miniature versions on wooden cocktail sticks (toothpicks).

SERVES 4
PREP 10 MINUTES
COOK 8–12 MINUTES

16 large raw king prawns
    (jumbo shrimp), peeled
    with tails intact
250g (9oz) halloumi, cut into
    2cm (¾ inch) cubes
1 chorizo sausage, cut into
    12 slices
a handful of coriander
    (cilantro), chopped
juice of 1 lime
steamed rice, couscous
    or pasta, e.g. orzo, to serve

MARINADE
2 tbsp olive oil
juice of 1 lime
1 tsp runny honey
2 garlic cloves, crushed
1 tsp smoked paprika

Soak 12 long wooden skewers in some water for 20–30 minutes. This will prevent them burning when you cook the kebabs in the griddle pan.

Make the marinade: mix all the ingredients together in a bowl until well blended. Add the prawns and stir gently until they are coated all over with the marinade.

Thread the prawns, halloumi and chorizo alternately onto the wooden skewers.

Lightly oil a large griddle pan and set over a medium to high heat. Cook the skewered prawns, halloumi and chorizo, a few at a time, for about 2 minutes each side until the prawns are uniformly pink and the halloumi is crisp and golden brown. Keep warm while you cook the remaining skewers.

Divide the skewers among four serving plates and sprinkle with the coriander (cilantro) and lime juice. Serve immediately with steamed rice, couscous or pasta.

HALLOUMI 'FISH AND CHIPS'

//

This is a bit of a cheat, but a delicious one nevertheless. Chunks of firm halloumi are fried in a crisp, light batter as a vegetarian fish substitute, and chunky potato chips are oven-baked for a healthy, low-fat alternative to French fries.

SERVES 4
PREP 15 MINUTES
COOK 25 MINUTES

600g (1lb 5 oz) potatoes,
    scrubbed and cut into
    chunky fingers
2 tbsp olive oil
½ tsp paprika
a pinch of cayenne or chilli
    powder
250g (9oz) halloumi, cut into
    fingers or large chunks
vegetable oil, for deep-frying
sea salt and freshly ground
    black pepper
tomato ketchup, hot sauce
    or tartare sauce, to serve

BATTER
100g (4oz/generous ¾ cup) plain
    (all-purpose) flour
1 tsp baking powder
150ml (5fl oz/2/3 cup) ice-cold
    beer or sparkling water
sea salt and freshly ground
    black pepper

Preheat the oven to 230°C (210° fan)/450°F/gas 8.

Toss the potatoes in the olive oil and spices. Add some salt and pepper and spread them out in a single layer on a large baking tray (cookie sheet).

Bake in the oven for about 25 minutes, turning them over once or twice, until crisp and golden brown.

Meanwhile, make the batter: whisk all the ingredients together in a large bowl until you have a smooth batter.

Pat the halloumi dry with kitchen paper (paper towels) so the batter will stick to it. Dip them into the batter.

Pour the oil in a deep-fat fryer, if you have one, or a large deep frying pan (skillet) to a depth of 2cm (¾ inch). Heat until it reaches 185°C (365°F). You can test this with a sugar (candy) thermometer or drop a tiny amount of batter into the hot oil and see if it immediately sizzles and floats. Add the halloumi, a few at a time (don't overcrowd the pan), and fry for about 2–3 minutes each side until really crisp and golden. Remove with a slotted spoon and drain on kitchen paper.

Serve the halloumi immediately with the potato chips and some tomato ketchup, hot sauce or tartare sauce.

BAKING

HALLOUMI BREAD WITH OLIVES AND ROSEMARY

//

There's something very soothing and satisfying about making your own bread. If you've never done it before you'll be delighted to discover that it's much easier than you thought. The olives and halloumi add a pleasing saltiness to this savoury loaf. Serve it with cheese, deli meats or just a simple salad.

MAKES ONE 500G
  (1LB 2OZ) LOAF
PREP 30 MINUTES
RISE 1¾ HOURS
COOK 30–35 MINUTES

500g (1lb 2oz/4 cups)
  strong white bread flour
2 tsp salt
2 tsp sugar
7g (¼oz) sachet fast-action
  dried yeast
250ml (9fl oz/generous 1 cup)
  lukewarm water
2 tbsp olive oil, plus extra
  for greasing

HALLOUMI, OLIVE AND
  ROSEMARY FILLING
1 small red onion, finely chopped
150g (5oz) stoned (pitted) black
  olives, coarsely chopped
leaves torn from a few sprigs
  of rosemary, chopped
150g (5oz) halloumi, diced

Sift the flour and salt into a large mixing bowl. Stir in the sugar and yeast and make a well in the centre. Pour in the lukewarm water and olive oil and mix together to form a soft dough.

Turn out the dough onto a lightly floured surface and knead well for 5–10 minutes until smooth and elastic. Place in a lightly oiled large bowl and cover with cling film (plastic wrap) or a clean tea towel. Leave in a warm place for about 1 hour until well risen and doubled in size.

Preheat the oven to 220°C (200°C fan)/425°F/gas 7. Lightly oil a baking tray (cookie sheet).

Knock the dough down with your fists and roll out to a rectangle. Sprinkle the red onion, olives, rosemary and halloumi over the top, then fold one-third over into the centre and the remaining third over the top. Press down firmly and then knead the dough to distribute the filling ingredients evenly throughout.

Shape the dough into a round loaf and place on the oiled baking tray. Cover loosely with oiled cling film (plastic wrap) and leave in a warm place for about 45 minutes until well risen.

Brush lightly with olive oil and bake in the oven for about 30–35 minutes until the loaf is golden brown and sounds hollow when you tap the bottom with your knuckles.

Cool on a wire rack and cut into slices to serve. The loaf will stay fresh in a bread bin or airtight container for up to 3 days.

HALLOUMI AND CHILLI-SWIRLED LOAF

///

There's nothing more wonderful than the aroma of freshly baked bread. This loaf is easy to make, but you can use an electric mixer with the dough hook attachment to take the hard work out of the kneading, if wished.

**MAKES ONE 500G
   (1LB 2OZ) LOAF**
PREP 20–25 MINUTES
RISE 1½ HOURS
COOK 30 MINUTES

500g (1lb 2oz/4 cups) strong
   white bread flour, plus extra
   for kneading
1 tsp salt
1 tsp sugar
7g (¼oz) sachet fast-action
   dried yeast
90ml (3fl oz/⅓ cup) lukewarm
   milk
150ml (5fl oz/⅔ cup) lukewarm
   water
2 tbsp olive oil, plus extra
   for greasing
milk or beaten egg, for glazing

HALLOUMI AND CHILLI FILLING
100g (4oz/¾ cup) grated
   halloumi
1 tsp dried oregano
1 red chilli, deseeded and diced

Sift the flour and salt into a large mixing bowl. Stir in the sugar and yeast and make a well in the centre. Pour the lukewarm milk, water and olive oil into the bowl and mix together to form a soft dough.

Turn out the dough onto a lightly floured surface and knead well for 5–10 minutes until smooth and elastic. Place in a lightly oiled large bowl and cover with cling film (plastic wrap) or a clean tea towel. Leave in a warm place for about 1 hour until well risen and doubled in size.

Preheat the oven to 220°C (200°C fan)/425°F/gas 7. Lightly oil or grease a 900g (2lb) loaf tin (pan).

Knock the dough down with your fists and roll out to a rectangle. Sprinkle the grated halloumi, oregano and chilli evenly over it. Roll up and shape into a loaf. Place in the loaf tin, with the seam underneath, then cover and leave in a warm place for about 25–30 minutes until the dough rises to the top of the tin.

Lightly brush the top of the loaf with milk or beaten egg and bake in the oven for 30 minutes until it's golden brown and sounds hollow when you tap the bottom with your knuckles.

Remove the loaf from the tin, cool on a wire rack and cut into slices to serve. The loaf will stay fresh in a bread bin or airtight container for up to 3 days.

CYPRIOT EASTER HALLOUMI BREAD

//

This bread is traditionally served at Easter. You can buy the mastic and mahlab powders at Greek delis or online. You can make the filling the day before you make the dough and cook the bread.

MAKES 12 BREADS
PREP 45 MINUTES, STAND
   OVERNIGHT, RISE 1¾ HOURS
COOK 30 MINUTES

125g (4½oz/½ cup) butter
2 medium free-range eggs
500g (1lb 2oz/4 cups) strong
   white bread flour
1 tsp baking powder
a good pinch of sea salt
1 tsp each mastic and mahlab
   (*mahlepi*) powder
7g (¼oz) sachet fast-action
   dried yeast
1 tsp caster (superfine) sugar
5 tbsp lukewarm milk
4 tbsp lukewarm water
beaten egg, for glazing
100g (4oz/⅔cup) sesame seeds

HALLOUMI AND RAISIN FILLING
500g (1lb 2oz/4 cups) grated
   halloumi
100g (4oz/generous ¾ cup)
   sultanas (golden raisins)
30g (1oz/¼ cup) semolina
1 tsp each of baking powder,
   mastic powder, mahlab powder
2 tsp dried mint
2 medium free-range eggs
2 tbsp milk

Make the filling: put the halloumi, sultanas, semolina, baking powder, mastic, mahlab and mint in a bowl and mix together. Beat the eggs and stir them into the mixture, along with the milk. Cover and leave to rest in the fridge overnight.

The following day, make the dough: beat the eggs and melt the butter. Sift the flour and baking powder into a large bowl and mix in the salt, mastic, mahlab, yeast and sugar. Make a well in the centre and pour in the melted butter, beaten eggs, lukewarm milk and water. Mix together to form a firm dough.

Knead the dough lightly for about 5 minutes – it's not supposed to be silky soft and elastic like a normal bread dough. Shape into a ball and place in a lightly oiled bowl. Cover with cling film (plastic wrap) and leave in a warm place for at least 1 hour until it rises and doubles in size.

Roll out the dough thinly on a lightly floured surface and cut out 12 circles, about 12cm (4½ inches) in diameter. Brush a little beaten egg over each circle and press it down firmly in the sesame seeds, spread out on a large plate. Turn the circles over, sesame side-down, and divide the filling among them, putting a little in the centre of each circle. Brush some beaten egg around the edge of the dough and bring the sides up around the filling, pinching them together to partially enclose it – some of the filling should be visible.

Arrange the breads on lightly greased baking trays (cookie sheets) and leave in a warm place for 30–45 minutes to rise. Preheat the oven to 200°C (180°C fan)/400°F/gas 6.

Bake in the oven for about 30 minutes until cooked and golden brown. Cool on a wire rack before eating.

HERBY HALLOUMI SCONES

//

These crisp-topped cheese scones are so versatile. You can not only serve them at teatime, but also with a bowl of vegetable soup for lunch, or with some cheese, celery and chutney or fig jam for a snack.

MAKES 6 SCONES
PREP 15 MINUTES
COOK 10–15 MINUTES

225g (8oz/2¼ cups) self-raising flour, plus extra for dusting
1½ tsp baking powder
½ tsp salt
½ tsp English mustard powder
50g (2oz/¼ cup) butter, diced, plus extra for greasing
1 tbsp black mustard seeds
a few sprigs of mint, finely chopped
125g (4½oz/1 cup) grated halloumi, plus extra for sprinkling
1 medium free-range egg, beaten
90–100ml (3–4fl oz/⅓ cup) milk, plus extra for brushing
2 tbsp sesame seeds
cayenne pepper, for dusting

Preheat the oven to 220°C (200°C fan)/425°F/gas 7. Lightly butter a baking tray (cookie sheet).

Sift the flour and baking powder into a large mixing bowl. Mix in the salt and mustard powder, then rub in the butter with your fingertips until the mixture resembles fine breadcrumbs. Stir in the mustard seeds, mint and halloumi.

Using a wide-bladed palette knife, gently stir the beaten egg into the flour and cheese mixture, together with enough milk to form a soft dough. Add more flour or milk if necessary to make it stick together without being too dry or too wet.

Dust a clean surface with flour and gently roll out the dough about 2cm (¾ inches) thick. Use a 6cm (2½ inch) fluted cutter to cut out rounds. Roll out the leftover dough and cut out some more rounds so you have approximately six scones.

Place the scones on the baking tray (cookie sheet) and brush them with milk. Sprinkle with sesame seeds and a little grated halloumi. Bake in the oven for 10–15 minutes until risen and golden brown.

Dust with cayenne and leave to cool slightly before serving warm. You can split and butter them, if wished.

HALLOUMI AND CARROT MUFFINS

///

These savoury muffins are best eaten warm on the day they are made, but they will keep in a sealed container for a couple of days and can be reheated. They are delicious for breakfast or brunch.

MAKES 12 MUFFINS
PREP 10 MINUTES
COOK 30 MINUTES

2 tbsp olive oil
1 red onion, finely chopped
a pinch of ground cumin
100g (4oz) baby spinach
  leaves, roughly torn
a few chives, snipped
250g (9oz/2½ cups)
  self-raising flour
1 tsp bicarbonate of soda
  (baking soda)
a good pinch of salt
2 medium free-range eggs,
  beaten
225g (8oz/1 cup) Greek
  yoghurt
125g (4½oz/1 cup) grated
  halloumi, plus extra
  for sprinkling
2 large carrots, grated
4 tbsp pumpkin seeds
2 tbsp pine nuts

Preheat the oven to 200°C (180°C fan)/400°F/gas 6. Line a 12-hole muffin tin (pan) with paper cases.

Heat the olive oil in a frying pan (skillet) over a medium heat and cook the red onion for 6–8 minutes until softened. Stir in the cumin and spinach and cook for 1 minute, then add the chives and leave to cool.

Sift the flour, bicarbonate of soda and salt into a large mixing bowl. Beat the eggs and yoghurt and stir into the flour with the cooled onion and spinach mixture. Fold in the halloumi, carrots, pumpkin seeds and pine nuts.

Divide the mixture among the paper cases and sprinkle lightly with grated halloumi. Bake in the oven for about 20 minutes until risen and golden brown.

Leave the muffins to cool in the pan for a few minutes and then transfer to a wire rack. Serve warm.

Tip: To test whether the muffins are cooked, insert a thin skewer into the centre – it should come out clean.

HALLOUMI PUFF PASTRY TWISTS

These delicious crisp, cheesy snacks are perfect for entertaining and parties.
Serve them with a glass of wine and a bowl of olives or as savoury dippers for tzatziki.

MAKES ABOUT 40 TWISTS
PREP 15 MINUTES
COOK 12 MINUTES

425g (14oz) pack ready-rolled
    puff pastry sheets (2 sheets)
flour, for dusting
125g (4½oz/1 cup) grated
    halloumi
100g (4oz/1 cup) grated Pecorino
    or Parmesan
a small bunch of chives, snipped
1 medium free-range egg, beaten
sea salt and freshly ground
    black pepper

Preheat the oven to 200°C (180°C fan)/400°F/gas 6.
Line two baking trays (cookie sheets) with baking parchment.

Unroll one of the pastry sheets onto a lightly floured surface.
Scatter nearly half of the grated cheeses over it. Sprinkle with
the chives and season with a little salt and pepper.

Fold the pastry in half to cover the cheesy filling and roll out
to the original size. Cut into strips 1cm (½ inch) wide and brush
lightly with beaten egg. Twist them three or four times. Repeat
with the remaining sheet of pastry.

Arrange the pastry twists on the baking trays and sprinkle with
the remaining cheese. Bake in the oven for about 12 minutes
until puffed up and golden brown.

Leave to cool completely before eating. You can store them
in an airtight container for 48 hours.

INDEX

//